Held In The Heavens Until. . .

Earl Paulk

Unless otherwise noted, all scripture quotations in this book are from **The New King James Version.**

Copyright 1985
K Dimension Publishers
Atlanta, Georgia

Printed in the United States of America
ISBN 0-917595-07-6

K Dimension Publishers

P.O. Box 7300 • Atlanta, GA 30357

ACKNOWLEDGEMENTS

I wish to thank the Publications Department of Chapel Hill Harvester Church for their daily efforts and continuing dedication to the Lord in the preparation of this book.

I thank Tricia Weeks for her most capable oversight and direction of the rewriting and editing of these manuscripts.

I deeply appreciate the faithfulness of our Editorial Staff—Gayle Blackwood, Chris Oborne and Gail Smith—as they converted verbatim transcriptions into workable manuscripts.

I thank Wes Bonner for his expertise in coordinating the technical aspects of publishing this book. I give special thanks to Donna Eubanks for typesetting; to Don Ross for layout and paste-up; and to Todd Cole for photography.

Finally, I am especially grateful for those who so willingly gave their time and skills to further the message of the Kingdom of God: Angela Hamrick, Linda Jacobson and Kae Rivenbark for transcribing; and Janis McFarland for proofreading.

May the seeds of the words herein bear much fruit for the glory of the Kingdom of God.

DEDICATION

DEDICATION

To my beloved sister, Joan Paulk Harris—

She lived and died and lives forever as a witness to the gospel of the Kingdom. She overcame every trial through the blood of the Lamb, the word of her testimony and loving not her life unto death. She lives today as a Kingdom intercessor, beholding the face of God, joining in intercession with all of creation, eagerly awaiting the manifestation of the sons of God.

And her memory chains me as a bond-servant pressing toward the glorious promise of the Lord:

That in the dispensation of the fullness of times He might gather together in one all things in Christ, both which are in heaven and which are on earth—even in him . . . (Ephesians 1:10)

INTRODUCTION

Mature Christians have an incredible sense of timing that is one of God's most precious gifts to them. They can hear God speaking to their spirits, "Go now!", "Wait," "Soon" and "I'm preparing you . . ." Too often Christians grasp genuine promises from the Lord which sound to them like "immediate events" only to eventually let go of those promises in confusion after long delays and numerous hindrances to fulfillment.

This frustration in individual experiences at seemingly senseless delays in realizing God's "reconciliation of all things" is very much the bewilderment commonly felt throughout the Church today. Did the Bridegroom really mean all the promises He made to us? After receiving His words whispered in our ears in a three-year courtship of love, even requiring obedience to death to assure His intentions, the Bride of Christ is left wondering why the wedding is postponed. The intense Bridegroom remains at the right hand of the Father "interceding for us." Why?

Many Christian leaders across denominational and doctrinal lines agree that we are in "the season" of Christ's second coming. Unfortunately, too few Christians realize that this event will never occur until the Bride of Christ grows to maturity. The Church's lack of preparation perpetuates a heartbreaking delay for generations. We wrestle daily in a cruel world of wars, famine, murder, deformity, dying children, drugs, horrible diseases without cures, broken homes, hopelessness and despair. Saints in both heaven and earth

vi

travail, crying, "How long? How long?" But in their sincere questions, too many Christians settle for silence by looking into the heavens and waiting for God to do something. They fold their hands and sing about "mansions in the sky" with resignation, or they tell themselves that "Jesus could come any second" to end all their problems.

The text of this book focuses on the Bride's mandatory preparation for a move of God that will culminate history. I am convinced that Jesus is lonely for His Bride, longing for an adequate witness, a standard, to fulfill His plan for all of creation. The Holy Spirit is stirring the hearts of God's people around the world to "make all things ready" for that event. The tragic realization of history is not the Bridegroom's centuries of delay, but realizing the Bride's lack of understanding her mission on earth.

Let me prepare you, the reader, for some startling challenges written on these pages. If you sat in my congregation at Chapel Hill Harvester Church in Atlanta, I would ask you to touch your ears and pray for God to anoint them to enable you to hear with understanding. I do recommend that you pray before you read this text. The Holy Spirit is "a teacher" leading us into all truth. Spiritual truth is spiritually discerned. Education, reasoning, logic and preconceived concepts of scripture may become either a hindrance or a help in understanding truth. I contend that revelation seldom follows logical paths or edifies people who think they already have all the answers.

Jesus spoke mysteries of the Kingdom in parables. After giving a series of parables describing the "kingdom of heaven," He said, "Therefore every scribe who has become a disciple of the kingdom of heaven is like a head of a household, who brings forth out of his treasure things new and old" (Matthew 13:2). As a man called by God to record Kingdom treasures that God speaks to this generation, I encountered a tremendous problem in selecting a title for this book. I know that "old treasures" often cause us to disregard or misunderstand the "new" ones. I value the "old treasures," but I am responsible to God for sharing "new treasures" with people who are searching for answers to the mysteries of God's Kingdom.

The dominant understanding of "Pentecost" in the Church is an "old treasure." Using the word "Pentecost" to title the message of this text would automatically exclude and divide Christian readers denominationally, experientially and doctrinally. We have defined the happening in Jerusalem at Pentecost in narrow concepts which contain many truths, but fall far beneath all the truth about God's intentions in sending us the Holy Spirit. I believe that "new treasures" concerning the meaning of Pentecost will point the Church responsibly, irrevocably toward the next great move of God in a unity that both restores and rekindles the fires of Pentecostal power in mighty Kingdom demonstration.

The Church's commitment to "witnessing" is an "old treasure." Beyond leading people to a personal confession of Jesus Christ as their Saviour is the "witness" principle. The "new treasure" witness is a demonstration of responsible Christianity in lifestyle. Two witnesses established truth throughout scripture in both the Old and New Testaments. Jesus sent out His disciples in pairs to witness and demonstrate Kingdom authority through their lifestyles. Peter and John demonstrated Kingdom witness after Pentecost in miraculous power and authority. Paul traveled with Barnabas and later with Silas in preaching and demonstrating the Kingdom to the Gentiles. Even a negative witness requiring judgment was made in the early Church through two witnesses, Ananias and Sapphira who lied to the Holy Spirit (Acts 5).

When, where and how did "witness" become a narrow concept of evangelism aimed solely at personal salvation? Connotations of the word "witness" in the minds of most Christians is far beneath the significance of "witness" according to God's plan for His covenant people. Everything Jesus did in His ministry became a "witness" to powers and principalities of darkness that God was establishing a new Kingdom on earth. Jesus' confrontation and victory over Satan is one witness—but God requires two! Jesus is the "firstfruit of many brethren." The Church must become that second witness—that "new treasure" witness—to signal in heavenly places that "His enemies have become His footstool" (Acts 2:35). An adequate witness is essential to the next great move of God.

Another essential ingredient to God's moving again throughout the earth is "Church unity." Most of our attempts at "unity" in the Church have grown from concepts that are "old treasure." We all agree in theory that the Body of Christ is one body. Where is the demonstration of that concept in reality? If Jesus prayed that we become one "so the world may know . . ." no wonder the world continues in darkness while the Church bickers among its members. The "new treasure" of unity in the Church has nothing to do with old ecumenical, organizational alliances. I don't criticize past efforts at unity or organizations which open dialogue among believers from various doctrinal persuasions. I only "test the fruit" to know that the oneness between Jesus and the Father has not been demonstrated yet among the people of God. I am also certain that the next move of God, like the move at Pentecost, requires one Spirit in one mind and one accord.

Prepare your heart to receive "new treasure" in preparation for when God will move again. Be willing to both "hear" and "do" as the Holy Spirit directs you. And as God confirms these words in your heart, teach them to your children, speak them in your conversations, live them in your circumstances and regard them as treasure from the Holy Spirit, giving those with "ears to hear" an important opportunity in history. I share this message with you as a steward of God's truth in personal brokenness and great spiritual triumph. To Him be the glory forever! Our King cometh!

TABLE OF CONTENTS

TABLE OF CONTENTS

Part 1

God's Intentions

1

THE MYSTERIES OF GOD

My sister Joan's death was not a time for me to acknowledge my own grief, but rather an opportunity to speak things that I know are the mind of the Lord. Joan's illness brought our family, as well as the membership of Chapel Hill Harvester Church in Atlanta, to a time when we had to practice what we preached. Sometimes simply preaching a gospel is too easy. When we actually live out what we preach, we demonstrate a true witness to the world.

Death. The word itself sounds so cruel. It jolts our sensibilities toward involuntary faith and speaks incomprehensible answers to our finite questions. We quote scripture passages, then ask ourselves what they really mean. We feel moments of panic with heartbreaking, cold realizations of our loss. Grief overwhelms us intermittently, yet unexpected joy, peace and astonishing promises surround us as we put the Comforter to the maximum test. Our capacity to receive His promises is also tested. Trust! Hope! Believe! These are such weighty words when we touch death through a life we've shared and adored.

She was forty-one, a beautiful woman, my baby sister Joan. Her three-year bout with cancer put all my doctrines and theological answers under intense scrutiny. She beat lymphoma in the first round, enjoying almost a year of remission. Throughout the first test I knew that God was leading me to wage a spiritual war that would bring certain victory.

I told Joan's children, Dana and Deanna, that their mother would not die during her first physical battle. God pressed me to claim that promise repeatedly. After praying about the matter, Joan, her husband, Donnie, who heads our television department, and I agreed that Joan would submit herself to the doctors' care by undergoing chemotherapy.

Many times I fought over Joan in toe-to-toe combat when powers and principalities attempted to take her life. I remember one night in her hospital room when the warfare was so intense that I insisted everyone else leave the room. I prayed for hours in the Spirit, waging an intense tug-of-war that only Joan and I could ever fully comprehend in the human realm of understanding. Describing the experience of confrontation with warlike spirits is impossible—though Joan attempted to tell the story many times to people close to her. I fought for Joan's life only in the power of the Lord and under His command. My efforts would have otherwise been futile, regardless of how many years I've preached the gospel, how greatly I loved my sister, or how much I wanted her to live.

God gave us a great gift in the short period of time Joan enjoyed "complete remission" status. She worked as a financial accountant in my office suite, always just a few steps down the hall from my desk. We shared daily the concerns, goals, disappointments and victories of the ministry at Chapel Hill Harvester Church. Joan pressed me to uncompromising boldness in the message God has called me to proclaim. She knew my weaknesses—my tendency to give things away; my overriding love for people; my great desire to withhold cutting, sharp truth which they needed to force them into spiritual confrontation and life-challenging choices.

Joan never allowed me to back away from the things God instructed me to preach. When I admonished God's people with "hard sayings," Joan shared my tears and my broken heart. We shared numerous prayers over people in trouble in my congregation. She knew the flesh, the emotions, the anointed spirit and the heartbeat of Chapel Hill Harvester Church. She was a "spiritual mother" among us. Joan diligently interceded for our failures and exhorted our strengths. I trusted her spirit completely.

God told me that Joan's physical battle was not over months before the tumor appeared inside her cheek in the late summer of 1984. Again we prayed about the treatment and felt that she should undergo chemotherapy for the second time. The battles were intense from the beginning. Her physical struggles paralleled battles in the ministry of our local church with precision timing. To deny some correlation between them would be foolish even for the most pronounced skeptic.

Scripture teaches "vicarious suffering." Although I will not attempt to explain mysteries of God without direct revelation from Him, I know that Joan's illness and death have tremendous implications for the entire ministry at Chapel Hill. The things God spoke to me about Joan's struggle, my spiritual dreams and the confirmations I have received leave me with indelible convictions and expectations.

Three major events marked Joan's message to Chapel Hill Harvester Church during the last few days of her life. One Sunday night she joined me on the platform to pray for healing of the infirmities among people in our congregation. She cried out to God in their behalf, praying for life to flow among them. I asked Joan whether she believed the message of the Kingdom enough "to love not her life unto death." Without any hesitation Joan said that she wanted the Kingdom to come in its fullness far more than she desired her physical healing.

I later received criticism from many people concerning that night, but I know that Joan's prayer was like a sweet aroma before God's throne. The next week was the last good report we had from her doctors. The spinal fluid was clear—no trace of cancer cells. I felt guarded emotions in our rejoicing, but I knew that God had honored Joan's petition for our people with a sign in her body. I was so grateful to the Lord.

Joan was furious on Easter Sunday morning because she was in the hospital and could not come to church. She felt much better and couldn't understand the doctor's caution in insisting she stay a few more days. Our family gathered in my office before the service to video-tape the grandchildren, nieces and nephews in their new Easter clothes for Aunt Joan to see. We tried to be dramatic and silly, hiding our tears off camera at knowing how much Joan wanted to be with us and missing her immensely.

That afternoon I participated at an anniversary service at Faith Memorial Assembly of God Church in Atlanta where my sister, Darlene, and her husband, Jimmy Swilley, minister. I rushed home to change clothes before going to the evening service at Chapel Hill to enjoy an Easter musical drama written by my middle daughter, Joy. My wife, Norma, told me to call the hospital immediately. Joan had some exciting news to share with me.

Overwhelming emotion electrified her voice. Jesus had visited Joan in the hospital room. He stood by her bed, took her hand and they talked and walked together. He told her of His loneliness for His Bride. He spoke directly to her concerning certain aspects of the ministry of Chapel Hill Harvester Church—specific insights concerning people who worked in this ministry. He spoke to her about "agape" love which will bring His Bride to the intimacy and fellowship which

He longs to share with her. She told me to take a message of "agape" love to the congregation.

The Easter drama presented that night, "The Rose," captured Jesus' heart in a way that moved the entire congregation to weeping. My daughter, Joy, had struggled with many inner conflicts and doubts when God told her to write a drama about Mary Magdalene's love for Jesus. Joy had obediently poured her life into the play—depicting Mary's own conflicts of separating her human desires from divine love for the Lord, realizing finally at His death the eternal meaning of His life. Joy, in the role of Mary Magdalene, and Sharalee Lucas, as Mary the mother of Jesus, sang a song called "The Rose," written by Dottie Rambo, about the crushing of Jesus for the world. One of the final songs in the drama was "I've Just Seen Jesus," written by Gloria Gaither, which proclaims the ecstasy of the disciples at Jesus' resurrection.

No one could deny the message or miss its significance for this church in Decatur, Georgia. Unexplainably, like Jesus, Joan Harris was a crushed rose with a permeating fragrance affecting all of our lives. Joan, like the disciples long ago, had just seen Jesus. After the visitation from the Lord in her hospital room, nothing else in her life really mattered except the glow of recalling her face to face encounter with Him.

Just after Joan's visitation, God spoke to me about "Operation Unity." I cannot fully explain what it means, how it will happen specifically, or why God put the call so immovably in my spirit. I only know that I am called and committed to provoke the Church

6

toward maturity and unity. In 1983 I wrote a book called **The Wounded Body of Christ** which began my firm commitment to the restoration of the Church. The same night that God put the words "Operation Unity" in my spirit, I experienced a release concerning my sister's struggle. The two events are synonymous within me. I cannot explain how or why, but I know that my love and protection for Joan and her significant battle press me to this momentous mission.

I immediately opened my spirit to hear and understand how God intends to unify His people. I began preaching a series called "The Jerusalem Happening" on April 21, 1985, a series which I continued until Pentecost Sunday, May 26. I told my congregation to begin praying about Pentecost Sunday which would be a landmark day at our church.

Meanwhile, God began to pour revelation into my spirit concerning the meaning of Pentecost. I contend that the demonstration of those messages has the potential of changing the world and bringing the Kingdom to earth as it is in heaven. I claim that conviction without pride or apology. I spoke as God spoke to me. The messages recorded in this book are for those who will receive what the Spirit is speaking to the Church in this hour. My responsibility is only obedience to God.

Pentecost Sunday was indeed a glorious day at our church in Atlanta. Expectancy hung like a canopy over us. Almost everyone in the church wore red clothing in celebration of Pentecost. I preached the tenth sermon in the "Jerusalem Happening" series that morning and felt a powerful anointing, unity and openness throughout the congregation. Worship in the church was incredible.

My oldest daughter, Becky, and her husband, Pastor Sam Lalaian, spent Pentecost Sunday at the hospital with Joan and her husband, Donnie. All day Joan would communicate with them as they praised and worshipped the Lord in unity. They would worship aloud together around her bed for long periods of time. Sam would ask her, "Are you tired, Joan? Do you want us to stop for awhile?" She would frown and grunt insistently, urging them to continue worshipping. She seemed to respond to nothing else, as if only praise to Jesus was worthy of any strength that remained in her fragile body.

The Sunday night service was very unusual. We enjoyed the presence of the Lord in what can only be described as a "Love Feast"! Evening services are usually lively at Chapel Hill Harvester Church, but that night was special in celebration, dancing, personal, one to one ministry in corporate love—all in one spirit, one place and one accord. People from the congregation lined up to embrace me, my brother Don, members of the Presbytery and each other. The service didn't even end as usual. Finally, we just paused, prayed and people began to leave. Ten minutes after the conclusion of the "Love Feast," Joan died.

Is "Operation Unity" simply the expression of a grieving brother trying to make sense out of personal tragedy and loss? Does "Operation Unity" represent an attempt to decipher the unexplainable mystery of "early" death for one so committed to the cause of God, one who seemingly had so much left to do? I only know that any attempt to back away from this message in resolution or in intimidation is impossible.

On Thursday, August, 1, 1985, God spoke to my spirit that He would "speak to me in the storm." I shared the strange words with several people, and even told the staff the next day that God was birthing a sermon in me about "God speaking in the storm." That evening I experienced a grieving in my spirit that caused me to weep without any explanation. I conducted a wedding and visited with several hundred beautiful people at a New Members' Dinner while feeling totally numb and heavy inside, hardly able to speak. I wanted to find a quiet place to search out the meaning of this strange, spiritual melancholy within me.

Within hours I received a telephone call that one of the most vital workers in the ministry at Chapel Hill, Rudy Price, had been flying as the First Officer on Delta Flight 191 which had crashed at the air terminal in Dallas in a violent storm. I rushed to be with Dawn, his wife, and their teenaged children, Mike and Christy, as they waited for news concerning the crash. Several other pastors joined me to share the shock and grief of the family who received the tragic news of Rudy's death.

Why did forty-two-year-old Rudy Price die? No one can answer that question, but I do know the message of the man's life. He lived "Operation Unity" in an ecumenical commitment that was an extraordinary example. Rudy was a member of Saint Peter and Paul's

Catholic Church. His wife, Dawn, is a member of Chapel Hill Harvester Church. Their family attended early Mass together and then came to Chapel Hill for morning worship at 10:00 a.m. every Sunday—in complete spiritual unity.

Rudy led the prison ministry at Chapel Hill Harvester with a commitment to the restoration of people whom society has condemned and forgotten. He recruited people to teach prisoners how to read, realizing that illiteracy was a major cause of daily frustration in driving numerous people to crime. Rudy wrote me long letters as updates on the prison ministry. Together we discussed concerns we shared about the universal Church. He faithfully attended our Wednesday staff luncheons every week, often giving reports to the "full time" staff concerning his "volunteer" ministry in which he invested numerous hours. All of us learned from him. He also came to leadership meetings, business meetings and appeared in a commercial for our television outreach ministry, Partners For the Kingdom.

Like Joan, Rudy understood the Church. He understood the reasons the pastors on our staff wear clerical collars and full vestments to serve the Eucharist. He walked, talked and lived "Operation Unity." Rudy knocked down walls and built bridges. He joined hands with any brother or sister naming the name of Jesus Christ. He ran to me with tears in his eyes after I visited with Father Scanlan at Steubenville University several years ago asking, "What happened, Bishop Paulk?" Rudy Price! God spoke to me in the storm and unity was the message of Rudy Price's life. Dawn Price symbolized Rudy's goal at his funeral by calling it "the whole loaf of bread."

God's Word teaches that in death, we find life. Jesus said, "Except a seed die, it abides alone . . ." We stand so finite before God with our own thoughts, our understanding, our opinions of what should and should not be. But in the Infinite are mysteries far above our mortal values. Paul said,

> *And I, brethren, when I came to you, did not come with excellence of speech or of wisdom declaring to you the testimony of God. For I determined not to know anything among you except Jesus Christ and Him crucified. I was with you in weakness, in fear, and in much trembling. And my speech and my preaching were not with persuasive words of human wisdom, but in demonstration of the Spirit and of power, that your faith should not be in the wisdom of men but in the power of God. However, we speak wisdom among those who are mature, yet not the wisdom of this age, nor of the rulers of this age, who are coming to nothing. But we speak the wisdom of God in a mystery, the hidden wisdom which God ordained before the ages for our glory, which none of the rulers of this age knew; for had they known, they would not have crucified the Lord of glory. But as it is written: "Eye has not seen, nor ear heard, nor have entered into the heart of man the things which God has prepared for those who love Him."*
> *(I Corinthians 2:1-9)*

Through recorded and ongoing prophetic revelation, we learn of things that we have never seen or heard. Revelation, given by those anointed and called of God to give direction to the Church, moves believers toward reality in the spiritual realm. Some events in human life are held in sacrament. Sacrament simply means "the mysteries" of the Church. If we knew everything, sacraments would be meaningless and unnecessary.

It is doubtless not profitable for me to boast. I will come to visions and revelations of the Lord: I know a man in Christ who fourteen years ago—whether in the body I do not know, or whether out of the body I do not know, God knows—such a one was caught up to the third heaven. And I know such a man—whether in the body or out of the body I do not know, God knows—how he was caught up into Paradise and heard inexpressible words, which it is not lawful for a man to utter. Of such a one I will boast; yet of myself I will not boast, except in my infirmities. For though I might desire to boast, I will not be a fool; for I will speak the truth. But I forbear, lest anyone should think of me above what he sees me to be or hears from me. (II Corinthians 12:1-6)

Paul tried desperately to relate spiritual visions he saw to the Church. Some of his visions were so far beyond natural comprehension that their meanings were held in mystery. The Apostle Paul spent his ministry talking about things that he had heard and seen in the Spirit.

When revelation becomes reality, we often remember mysteries God has previously spoken to our spirits. Jesus gave us some examples. He talked about the destruction of the temple. He said, "This temple can be destroyed, and in three days, I will rebuild it." That remark seemed outrageous to those who heard His words. Jesus often spoke in mysteries and parables because the world would not receive His message. He taught His disciples in mysteries and parables, assuring them that only spiritual minds could comprehend His words.

Natural understanding always labels God's mysteries as "foolishness." When Jesus Christ was risen from the dead, the disciples remembered His words concerning raising the temple and finally they understood that Jesus referred to His own body, not to a man-made temple (John 2:22). When revelation becomes reality, spiritual minds always remember the mysteries which God spoke to them.

Jesus rode triumphantly into Jerusalem on a donkey. That event announcing His kingship seemed a strange occurrence until the disciples remembered that the prophet said that the Messiah would ride into Jerusalem upon an ass (Zechariah 9:9). Revelation became reality. They remembered the mysteries God had spoken only after the event.

Another occasion when the disciples finally comprehended previous revelation from the Lord is found in Luke's gospel.

Now on the first day of the week, very early in the morning, they, and certain other women with them, came to the tomb bringing the spices which they had prepared. But they found the stone rolled away from the tomb. Then they went in and did not find the body of the Lord Jesus. And it happened, as they were greatly perplexed about this, that behold, two men stood by them in shining garments. Then, as they were afraid and bowed their faces to the earth, they said to them, "Why do you seek the living among the dead? He is not here, but is risen! Remember how He spoke to you when He was still in Galilee, saying, 'The Son of Man must be delivered into the hands of sinful men, and be crucified, and the third day rise again.'" And they remembered His words. (Luke 24:1-8)

Many truths of God are yet held in mystery. Sometimes Christians have a tendency to forget that we do not know all the truths of God. Some truths are yet held in sacrament. The Eucharist is a mystery, often defined as transubstantiation. Others say that partaking of communion is only symbolic. The truth is that the meaning of the Eucharist is held in mystery yet to be revealed. Often we obey God's instructions without understanding fully the significance of our obedience.

We are still seeking answers to many mysteries in the Church. We sometimes speak as if we have all the answers when in fact, we really don't. Let me illustrate some mysteries. What about death? Where is my sister Joan? Where is Rudy Price? Everyone who reads the Bible knows that it says, "To be absent from the body is to be present with the Lord." But geographically, where are departed saints? Are they on earth in another realm? Are they in the hearts of their families and friends? Are they in a third or a seventh heaven? Are they in another "heavenly" dimension? Where are they? No one knows. We simply hold them in a mystery, satisfied with knowing that they are "with the Lord."

All the arguments that we may make—what happens at death; how we prepare for the return of Christ; whether we wait until the Church gets grown, or we go to heaven as babes; whether the Church is raptured, or whether we wait on earth to meet Christ— all those truths are held in mystery.

What about the redemption of the body? I have read doctrines of great men in Church history. I have spent much of my life reading theological, philosophical theories. The fact of the matter is that no one actually knows. We know by faith. We live by faith. Faith is the substance that gives confidence to Christians. But areas of faith are still not the same as sure reality. "Eye has not seen, ear has not heard . . ." Some mysteries are indescribable; therefore, we rest our case by saying, "We are people of faith." We have feelings, insights, visions, revelations and dreams from God that convince us of truth. We believe God's Word. But those same convictions, judged by the natural mind in a courtroom, cannot be proven. Even if one dies for his beliefs, his strong convictions are not viable as proof in a courtroom.

Much of God's authority on earth is held in mystery. We still have so much to learn in these areas. Is the role of the Church one of "a custodian" of grace? Does the Church actually have the power to bombard the gates of hell? Is the Church "a witness before principalities and powers" (Ephesians 4:10)? Is the Church a witness to the world through testimony, or must she demonstrate the gospel to every creature? All of these speculations sound great, intriguing and accurate. We don't really know how these things occur. We can only preach and teach truths we learn in God's Word, as the Spirit brings understanding through revelation.

The fact is that we only know what God reveals to us. The writer of Deuteronomy said, "The secret things belong to God, and to those to whom God will reveal it"

(Deuteronomy 29:29). Amos 3:7 says, "Surely the Lord does nothing, unless He reveals His secrets to His prophets." Joel prophesied that old men dream dreams and young men have visions. Christians continue to argue and debate various doctrines, yet we really don't know indisputable answers to questions requiring faith.

How do we overcome? By the blood of the lamb? The redemptive process of Christ? The revealed word of God? The power of our testimony? Must we all arrive at a place of saying, "I love not my life unto death!"? Paul said, "I would count myself accursed if I could win my brethren." We can debate these matters. Someone may even seem to win the debate. The truth is that all of these issues are held in mystery or we wouldn't need faith. Faith alone is the arena that does not require absolute, concrete substance in our finite understanding.

"How dare you air your disputes before the world?" the apostle said. Men of God should meet behind closed doors to discuss the Word of God concerning scriptural areas that are still held in mystery. Then we won't sound so authoritative and divided. Let the world see only a united people bought by the blood of Jesus Christ.

I know I hear from God. That statement sounds terribly presumptuous, but everything I heard from God concerning my sister's illness has been documented with more than two witnesses. I heard from the Lord that Joan would either die or she would fully recover on Pentecost Sunday. I had no doubt in my mind of that promise. I knew the Lord had spoken it. I knew her life and death had far more meaning than simply a battle due to the devilish disease of cancer.

I have never known a person who loved peace more than Joan Harris. Never! As a matter of fact, in her dying moments, if someone in spiritual conflict came into her room, Joan's eyes would start moving quickly and she would look troubled. To the moment of her death, Joan was extremely sensitive to conflicts surrounding her.

Joan and I had a private agreement. That agreement was concerning a united ministry—no black church, no white church, or any prejudice within the church. Our consuming desire stated that no compromise would prevent the ministry at Chapel Hill Harvester Church from proclaiming unity and maturity in the Body of Christ.

Power comes through unity. Pentecost could not even take place until the disciples were in total agreement. Let's find areas of unity! John 20:31 puts it very succinctly, "These things are written that you may believe that Jesus is the Christ." The truth that "Jesus is the Christ" must never be controversial among us. He will become either our stumbling block or cornerstone. No mystery concerning Jesus' identity should ever divide His Church. That issue is not a sacrament. We must never vary from that truth.

Error concerning Jesus' identity opens doors to many other religions, erroneous ideas of justifying "good" people, humanistic philosophies and moral teachings which contradict pure Christianity. To compromise Jesus' identity is to lose the truth that Jesus lived and died to save us. He is the chief cornerstone to the Greek and to the Jew. To deny Him is to deny God's total plan of incarnation. Therefore, we must stand solidly together to proclaim that Jesus is the Christ! No negative response to that conviction can possibly surface among true Christians.

Secondly, God has always wanted a people. Adam and Eve were created as "offspring of God" (a term recorded in Acts 17:28) because He wanted a people. I believe that God created them to correct problems in the universe. When they failed, God began "the seed" principle. This plan promised that through the seed of a woman, God would redeem "that which was lost." That principle is one of God's mysteries. We can build our lives and ministry upon the truth that God wants a people. Call them "peculiar," call them "strange," call them "a priesthood," call them "kings and priests," God wants a people. He describes them as "a people who were not a people." If they were a people that we could define by their race or their geographical location, they would not be "a people who were not a people."

God is looking for "a people who were not a people," with only the indwelling Holy Spirit as their requirement. God wants a people who will be His sanctuary, a dwelling place where His presence can abide in worship. He seeks people to worship Him in Spirit and in truth. Let's put down stakes of unity. Jesus is the Christ; God wants a people who will embody His presence and know Him.

The third stake is recognizing the Church that Jesus built. He clearly told us how He would build it. "Who do men say that I am?" The disciples said, "Some say You are this prophet and some say You are another prophet." Jesus looked squarely in the eyes of Peter as only Jesus could do, "Peter, what do you say?" Peter replied, "You are the Christ, the Son of the living God!" Jesus exclaimed, "On that revelation I will build My church and hell cannot stop it."

The Church is built upon the revelation that Jesus is the Christ. When the universal Church proclaims Christ as the only truth, unity is inevitable. Many "closet" Christians have never proclaimed that Jesus is the Christ. They must eventually come forward to manifest unity in God's Church.

The fourth stake that can bring unity is that Jesus will come again. All the methods of His return and speculation surrounding this truth are really not important. Different views of end time events are not going to change the reality of Jesus' return. Jesus will come again. We have some revealed truth to guide us. Matthew 24:6 says not to look at all the signs such as earthquakes, famines and pestilences. Many sermons have erroneously dwelled on those scriptures. I built sermons for years on earthquakes, famine and pestilence. Jesus instructed us not to be concerned about those problems, but I failed to read the scripture carefully. Jesus taught that when the gospel of the Kingdom has been demonstrated to the world and a standard is set by which God can judge the world, then

Christ can come again.

Jesus will return when we become a witness to powers and principalities. This principle is not a theory, mystery or sacrament. We may not fully comprehend how this witness occurs, but we are certain that it does. Paul clearly stated in Ephesians 3:10, "When we have made a witness to the principalities and powers."

We have confused "testimony" with "witness." We thought preaching to every creature was "witnessing," but that is not true. The dual witness in the Bible is very clearly defined as demonstrating God's truth in lifestyle. The "witness" principle was established when Jesus sent out seventy witnesses to live among people and teach them about His Kingdom through demonstration of His teaching (Luke 10).

A few days before Joan died, she talked about "a host." I was thrilled because I thought she saw an angelic host. She shook her head, "No!" I immediately understood that she was not referring to angels. The Spirit of the Lord said to me. "Read Psalm 27." I read, "Though an army should encamp against me." Joan responded, "Yes," that is what she meant." The frown on her face had indicated "a host against me." She turned her head and looked in another direction saying, "Witnesses." I asked her, "A cloud of witnesses, Joan?" She answered, "Yes." We are encompassed about with a cloud of witnesses.

Joan saw something like the servant of the great prophet saw when he said, "God, open the eyes of my servant and let him see." The servant's eyes were opened and he saw chariots rushing around him. A host encamps against God's army, but we are also surrounded by witnesses to God's righteousness. Joan smiled when I said, "Joan, we are on the winning side." The world she saw clearly in those last few days and weeks, few of us have ever seen. I do know that Joan saw many things in the spiritual realm.

My son-in-law, Steve, told the story of going out to Stone Mountain to run the morning after Joan died. He prayed, "Lord, I would like to communicate with Joan." I understand the dangers of seances and all the prostitutions and counterfeits of supernatural communication. But for every counterfeit, a reality exists. Moses and Elijah stood with Jesus as He was transfigured. Stephen, as he was being stoned, saw Jesus in the heavenlies. The rich man begged to send someone from the dead back to earth to warn his brothers. Interaction between the worlds of the natural and spiritual happens according to scripture.

Steve simply wanted some communication with Joan's spirit. He thought that talking to himself would bring back memories of some things that Joan had said to him. But Steve said that the Spirit of the Lord quickened his spirit saying, "No, I will grant a spiritual communication." Steve said he could hear the voice of Joan's spirit saying to him, "Steve, it is great over here! Everything we regarded as mystery—things we have been preaching and teaching and trying to understand—I understood instantly. I completely understand redemption—all those things I wondered about, I understand! Now, I see." Paul said, "We shall know fully even as we are known." Joan said, "I see it now, Steve. The place, the dimension in which I exist now is beyond anything I can describe." The Apostle Paul said, "I cannot describe it."

About the time that Steve thought their communication was going to end, Joan said with almost a hesitation, "But oh, Steve, to see Him, to see Him!" Paul also said it, ". . . to know Him is my greatest achievement."

I believe that on the other, eternal side, Joan is experiencing the reality of all the mysteries that we preach and teach and believe in God's Church. She joins all those under the altar who cry, "How long, how long?" Joan is saying to us, "Blessed be the name of our God! The Church is winning! I stand here as a witness to that fact." Call it my "fantasy," but somehow, I think Joan is skipping around in the corridors of glory. With her beautiful, tapered little fingers, her hand stretches out and she says, "Come on, Church! What you have is real! Do not compromise! Do not back off! Do not let the systems of this world confuse you! This is reality." And I know in Joan's own way with her cute, little, dimpled smile, she adds, "See, I got here first!"

A heavenly choir sings now with a new soprano voice. Every time we worship, Joan worships also. If the angels have the right to celebrate over one sinner who is saved, Joan has that right also. Every time we have a victory, she has a victory. If Joan's family and friends do not live out her convictions in that spirit, what a tragedy that will be. The memory of my sister Joan's life will become a challenge and a motivation. Those of us who knew Joan will now respond to our own challenges in the days ahead with the example of her unshakable faith.

So many aspects of faith are sacramental and mysterious until we face harsh realities of life and ask ourselves, "Is there a better way than this?" We have hope, and we have love that even death cannot separate. Neither life nor death nor powers nor principalities can separate us from the love of God. We are promised eternal things by faith. Faith is a mystery in sacramental truth, but faith works—even in death.

Kingdom faith carries us throughout life and makes the world systems tremble. The world does not tremble at hearing our great theories. The world does not tremble when the Church produces a best-selling song or album or book. The world trembles when it sees the Church as one, with a unity that will work in either peace or chaos, joy or sorrow, life or death.

We do not play games with the Kingdom message. We mean what we say with our lives every day. We are called to make a difference in the world, but that difference only becomes reality out of genuine unity in Jesus Christ.

2

THAT WHICH WAS LOST

Who was Jesus Christ? Jesus spoke of Himself as "the son of Abraham." What does that identity mean? Jesus never said, "I am the son of Moses." He said, "I am the son of Abraham."

Jesus also described Himself as the "light of the world." The earth, in its original state, was without form and void until God created light. "In the beginning was the Word, and the Word was with God, and the Word was God . . . In Him was life, and the life was the light of men. And the light shines in the darkness . . ." (John 1:1,4,5).

Jesus said of Himself, "I am truth." He did not merely say that He spoke truth; He said He was truth—

the revelation of truth. He came to set man free from earthly attachments, not from the world God made, but from the "systems" of the world. He is the Truth that frees us to live out our fullest potential.

Jesus said, "I am the way." The way to where? Where was He going? Where does He want us to go? To accept Jesus Christ is to begin that way toward fulfilling all the potential God has ordained for our lives. Some people live the spiritual life of a zombie. They were told that they didn't need to pursue God any further than the salvation experience.

Important questions concerning Jesus' identity must be answered. Until we address them, we exist as a group of people who are put to sleep by confessing something we have never activated in our lives. God has called His Church to move powerfully with the Spirit in "His way." Therefore, we must be alert to God's revelation to us and respond with our lives.

When we understand the full implication of the Jerusalem happening, we will begin to be totally new people. Everything we do will totally respond to the happening at Jerusalem. "What does this mean?" people asked on the day of Pentecost. Have we ever really asked that question? If we go to church, study God's Word and pray without experiencing a difference in our lives, we have never understood that "Jesus Christ is the way" of power available to us.

I am a third-generation Pentecostal and I never intend to be disrespectful to the fathers of Pentecost. Although they had genuine experiences of the Holy

Spirit, they did not fully understand the responsibility of receiving the baptism in the Holy Spirit. One of God's patterns is to give a tremendous experience first, then explain it later. The apostles did not have the slightest idea what they received on the day of Pentecost. They simply obeyed Jesus' instructions—they went to the upper room, came into one accord, and waited obediently until the Holy Spirit fell. When the Spirit fell on them, they still did not know why they had received it. That inner power began to activate something resident within them. They went down into the streets to preach "Jesus Christ." Within weeks after the Jerusalem happening, the apostles' words began to turn cities upside down because of the power of the Holy Spirit. Where did we lose that same power and zeal?

The power of Pentecost is not an experience to hoard within the walls of a church. The Holy Spirit was not given to produce an emotional high or to release frustrations by making us jump up and down, scream and talk in tongues. Emotional excitement is not even close to the purpose of the Holy Spirit. When the apostles were empowered with this heavenly visitation, they immediately rushed out into the streets. They began to change their society and influence their world. Persecution erupted from those who were envious of the power they sensed in the apostles.

But the Jews who were not persuaded, becoming envious, took some of the evil men from the marketplace, and gathering a mob, set all the city in an uproar and attacked the house of Jason, and sought to bring them out to the people.

27

But when they did not find them, they dragged Jason and some brethren to the rulers of the city, crying out, "These who have turned the world upside down have come here too. Jason has harbored them, and these are all acting contrary to the decrees of Caesar, saying there is another king—Jesus." (Acts 17:5-7)

The authorities became frightened. They perceived that the "sheep" were stronger than the "wolves." Jesus admonished us to be as "wise as serpents," but our strategy must be ministering as lambs. When we understand that God's purposes will be fulfilled through the power He has given to us, the world will indeed become afraid of the lambs!

The story of Zacchaeus reveals a great truth which I believe has been overlooked. After Zacchaeus came down from the tree and entertained Jesus at His house, he said to Jesus, "Look, Lord, I will give half of my goods to the poor. If I have taken anything from anyone by false accusation, I restore fourfold" (Luke 19:8). To Zacchaeus, salvation meant affirmative action—doing something. Salvation was more than repeating a few words inviting Jesus into his heart, then going his way without acting on his confession. People are deceived and misled if they think spiritual regeneration ends with salvation. Christianity is far more than that.

Zacchaeus had done things he should not have done. He responded to Jesus by saying nothing about "forgiveness of sins" or "believing on the Lord Jesus Christ." When he met truth, Zacchaeus said, "I'll straighten up my life. I'll pay back what I have taken. I will let people know that I have been with You by the action of my life." Jesus said something very important to him: "Today salvation has come to this house" (verse 9). Jesus did not say, "Repeat after me, 'I believe that you are Jesus Christ.' " Jesus said, "Because of what you have done today, Zacchaeus, salvation has come to your house."

Jesus continued, ". . . for the Son of Man has come to seek and to save that which was lost" (verse 10). What is the interesting word in that verse? Jesus did not say "to seek and save **those who** are lost." He said, "**that which** was lost." Salvation addresses "that" which was lost! When we find out what was lost, we will know the full meaning of salvation. We must find out what was lost so we'll discover what Jesus came to reclaim.

The key to understanding God, Jesus Christ and the Jerusalem happening on the day of Pentecost is to find "that which was lost." After Jesus had spoken to Zacchaeus, "because He was near Jerusalem," He spoke a parable about the Kingdom.

Jesus had to bring enlightenment because people thought the Kingdom of God would appear immediately. The parable concerned a nobleman who went into a far country to receive a kingdom for himself—something that was lost. What is Jesus' mission? He came saying, "We're going to recover something that's been lost."

Jesus immediately focused on the problem. "But his citizens hated him, and sent a delegation after him

29

saying, 'We will not have this man to reign over us' "
(Luke 19:14). Many times rebellion is still very much
our attitude today. By our words and actions, we effectively say, "We will not submit to any kind of rule or
authority. We're not going to do what **you** say to do.
We're going to do what **we** want to do!"

The rest of the parable gives insights on how the
servants regained the lost kingdom. They began to **do**
things: to plan, sow and reap the benefits of their
investments. They began to make things happen. They
were not just "hearers" of the Word—they were "doers"
as well. They began to recover that which was lost by
sowing and reaping—God's strategy of recovering that
which was lost.

Immediately after speaking the parable about the
lost kingdom, Jesus went to Jerusalem, mounted a
donkey and rode into town as a king. He was saying by
demonstration, "We've lost something. I'm going to
show you how to regain it."

"Lost" has little to do merely with individual salvation (Luke 19:10). Does that mean it is not important
that we be saved? I didn't say that! But we can be
"saved" according to the old interpretation and never
do anything to recover the Kingdom of God. Salvation
alone doesn't threaten the devil's kingdom. Satan
wants Christians to say, "I'm saved," then sit down
and wait for Jesus to return.

People of Jesus' day had the same mentality. They
were quite willing to let Jesus "do it all" for them. But
Jesus said, "Something is going to happen in Jerusa-

lem. When it happens, I will transfer My authority and power to you. You'll become My witnesses in the world." The world is going to learn what being "a sheep" is all about. A growing sheepfold of God is going to begin to touch the world in ways we cannot imagine.

Jesus began to demonstrate a new kind of Kingdom. He allowed people to call Him "a King." He challenged religious exercises that had become opiates to the people. He said, "This temple is supposed to be My house, My habitation, My place of interaction with My people. You've made it nothing more than a merchandising market!"

Who is this man who called Himself "truth," "light," "the way"? Who is this man who announced the beginning of a new Kingdom while He sat upon a donkey? In the beginning of the Apostle John's gospel, he proclaimed this man to be the Word made flesh. Who did John the Baptist say this man was? John cried out in the wilderness, "Make straight the way of the Lord." "The next day John saw Jesus coming toward him, and said, 'Behold! The Lamb of God who takes away the sin of the world!' " (John 1:29). Can we define "the sin of the world"? Few people have ever asked themselves what "the sin of the world" is.

We will never comprehend why the Lamb has come until we define the sin of the world. We must understand what we've lost if we expect to regain it. That problem is exactly where the Church is today. For the most part we preach a message without understanding. No wonder the Bible said that the mark of the last days would be the deception of even the "very elect."

What is the sin of the world? The sin of the world is "that which was lost" in the Garden. Events in the Garden of Eden give us clues as to the sin of the world. Jesus would never have come without the act of rebellion in the Garden. I will not debate whether the Son of God would have come if Adam and Eve had been obedient to God. The Bible says that He was "slain before the foundation of the world in the heart of God." Jesus totally depicted the character of God. But Jesus would never have had to die for sin without disobedience in the Garden.

"God so loved the world . . ." (John 3:16). God loved us in spite of the sin and rebellion of the world. Oddly enough, the sin of the world was not fleshly sins as we might think. Fleshly sins are only symptoms of the rebellion of the world. Lust, cheating, lying and stealing may be manifested in rebellious people, but that is not the sin of the world. The sin of the world is rebellion against God's authority and God's Kingdom.

We find a very interesting description of Jesus in Luke 4:1. "Then Jesus, being filled with the Holy Spirit . . ." Surely Jesus must have already had the Holy Spirit. If so, why did He have to be filled with the Spirit? Did He have power that is not available to us? The answer to that question is what the Jerusalem happening is all about.

Then, Jesus, being filled with the Holy Spirit, returned from the Jordan and was led by the Spirit into the wilderness, being tempted for forty days by the devil. And in those days He ate nothing, and afterward, when they had

32

ended He was hungry. And the devil said to Him, "If You are the Son of God, command this stone to become bread." (Luke 4:1-4)

Notice that the devil said, "**If** You are the Son of God . . ." Many people assume the devil already knew that Jesus was the Son of God. How did he know? Jesus had to do certain things before even Satan could know who He was. How many people did Satan ask if they were the Son of God before he asked Jesus? He might even have asked Abraham or Moses. But one important insight was revealed to us when Satan said to Jesus, "If You're the Champion God's going to send; if You are the Son of God, then command this stone to become bread." The devil knew that only the Son of God could do that.

Notice Jesus' demonstration of the Lamb spirit. The "wolf" spirit would have turned the stone into bread. But Jesus—weak, weary and near starvation—answered, "It is written, 'Man shall not live by bread alone, but by every word that proceeds out of the mouth of God.' " Satan must have staggered back in shock. "I'm not accustomed to this kind of warfare. Why didn't He grab a sword? Why didn't He come at me gritting his teeth? No! I don't know how to handle this. If you are the Son of God, show me your power!" Jesus' power was in His self-control, His ability to live out and demonstrate that He was in command by obeying God's voice.

Then the devil, taking Him up on a high mountain, showed Him all the kingdoms of the world in a moment of time. And the devil said to Him, "All this authority I will give You, and their glory; for this has been delivered to me, and I give it to whomever I wish. Therefore, if You will worship before me, all will be Yours." And Jesus answered and said to him, "Get behind Me, Satan! For it is written, 'You shall worship the Lord your God, and Him only you shall serve.'" (Luke 4:5-8)

The devil was basically speaking the truth when he said to Jesus, "I've got all the authority in this earth." How did he get that authority? Satan could say, "All authority that I have in the world, I received because man gave it to me. He gave it to me in the Garden. I took authority because man was disobedient to God." The first Adam lost his authority by rebellion, which is the sin of the world. Satan said, "Jesus, I'm going to give You this authority. When I do, You will reign next to me." Thousands and thousands of religious people have accepted that offer. Every time Christians participate in any act of disobedience against God's revelation today, we effectively deliver God's authority into Satan's hands all over again.

Then he brought Him to Jerusalem, set Him on the pinnacle of the temple, and said to Him, "If You are the Son of God, throw Yourself down from here. For it is written: 'He shall give His angels charge over You, to keep You,' "and, 'In their hands they shall bear You up, lest You dash Your foot against a stone.'" And Jesus answered and said to him, "It has been said, 'You shall not tempt the Lord your God.'" Now when the devil had ended every temptation, he departed from Him until an opportune time. Then Jesus returned in the power of the Spirit to Galilee, and news of Him went out through all the surrounding region.

34

And He taught in their synagogues, being glorified by all. (Luke 4:9-15)

Note that Satan did not end Jesus' temptations—he only departed "until an opportune time." Every opportunity Satan gets, he is still on the job. He will never admit he is defeated.

Jesus faced the ruler of this world. The new Kingdom which He came to establish collided head-on with the kingdom of this world, already established through Satan. Jesus came to recover those things that had been lost to the devil. Jesus and the devil had to confront each other. The devil was in charge of world systems and Jesus came to establish another system through God's plan of recovery.

God's new plan is what Jesus meant by seeking "that which was lost." Jesus' confrontations with the devil announced to the enemy, "You are now the god of this world, but I have come with a new system from God Himself. Now we going to see which one of these systems wins."

Jesus went back to Nazareth where He had grown up, took the Word of God, and read from the prophet Isaiah:

The Spirit of the Lord is upon Me, because He has anointed Me to preach the gospel to the poor. He has sent Me to heal the brokenhearted, to preach deliverance to the captives and recovery of sight to the blind, to set at liberty those who are oppressed, to preach the acceptable year of the Lord. (Luke 4:18-19)

That scripture was Jesus' proclamation of the method He would use to correct the sin of the world—rebellion—and recover that which was lost: preaching the gospel to the poor and making them rich; preaching healing to the brokenhearted and comforting their hearts; bringing deliverance to those who were captives by confronting them with truth; giving recovery of sight to those who were blinded by the gods of this world (mammon); and preaching the acceptable year of the Lord. That process of recovery is the reason we were given power and authority through the happening at Jerusalem.

What had been lost? Communication with God was lost. The recovery is praying in the Spirit. Pentecost was necessary because communication was lost and God said that from the Kingdom within—where the Holy Spirit dwells—a recovery of that communication would be restored.

What else was lost in rebellion in the garden? Self-identity was lost. Eve must have been a very lonely person walking through that garden wondering, "Who am I? Adam, why were we put here?" Adam may have responded, "Who am I, Eve? I don't know what I'm supposed to do. I look at my hands, but I don't know what to do with them."

We ask God why He allows war, strife, havoc and disease. Do we just live seventy years, poke a little money in the bank, then pay it out for cancer and toothaches? Is that what life is about? Lost from paradise . . . Adam wondered, "I'm not quite sure what I'm supposed to do in this world now."

"But, Adam, you were made to be a Son of God." "Oh, but I don't understand what you mean by that term, Eve. My mind has been blinded, confused. I don't even understand who I am." How many people don't have the slightest idea why they are living? They think life is playing another game of tennis, hitting another golf ball or going on another shopping spree. What are we doing in this lost paradise? What is our mission?

We've lost communication and the ability to know who we are. We have lost the "fruit of innocence." Suddenly, Eve said, "I don't feel comfortable, Adam. The things we used to enjoy in God's presence don't feel right anymore. Something has gone wrong. I'm naked, I tell you." Adam said, "I never heard that word before. What do you mean? I feel as you do, Eve—something is wrong." The fruit of innocence had been lost.

Homosexual activities mean that people are lost. Marriage relationships fail because people don't understand covenant unity. Discord in relationships means people are lost. "Why do I feel like I feel? I am naked. I am uncovered. I want things I shouldn't have." We've lost the fruit of innocence. God said to me, "They lost the fruit of innocence which came in obedience to My will. Once Adam and Eve chose disobedience, they lost the joy, peace and love of righteousness."

What else was lost? Confidence was lost in the Garden because of guilt. Confidence before God is absolutely necessary to be able to say, "I put myself totally into the hands of God." If we don't have confidence in God, we easily move in wrong directions. How do we get confidence before God? We must learn to enter humbly before Him saying, "God, what are You saying? I don't want to miss You, God."

Finally, Adam and Eve lost their power to command the earth. God had told Adam and Eve, "Speak to creation around you. You bring forth life. You name the birds and beasts. You take dominion, command the earth around you." But they lost that command. Now the world runs by forms and systems. Life is filled with heartaches and sorrows. Society is turbulent—it's a "dog eat dog" world in confusion. Should we send arms to Central America? Should we send grain to starving nations? Should we support the United Nations? Should we increase nuclear arms? Should we feed the Ethiopians? Man lost control of the earth! We can't command the domain God gave us the authority to command.

> *Then He went down to Capernaum, a city of Galilee, and was teaching them on the Sabbaths. And they were astonished at His teaching, for His word was with authority. Now in the synagogue there was a man who had a spirit of an unclean demon. And he cried out with a loud voice, saying, "Let us alone! What have we to do with You, Jesus of Nazareth? Did You come to destroy us? I know You, who You are—the Holy One of God!" But Jesus rebuked him saying, "Be quiet, and come out of him!" And when the demon had thrown him in their midst, it came out of him and did not hurt him. So they were all amazed and spoke among themselves, saying, "What a word this is! For with authority and power He commands the unclean spirits, and they come out." (Luke 4:31-36)*

How did Jesus speak? With authority! Kingdom

authority was lost. Spiritual authority terrifies rebellious spirits! When we teach about spiritual authority, rebellious spirits begin to cry, "Uh, oh! We'd better get away from here! I don't want that man's authority! I want my own authority! I am going to do my own thing and think through what He's saying. If I decide it's the Word of God, I'll tiptoe back in." Oh, no, you won't! Once you make a conscious decision before God, I promise that decision becomes an eternal, accountable choice.

Jesus went to Capernaum to minister with authority. When He rebuked the demon, He didn't even need to call the man's name. Who was Jesus actually confronting? He was confronting another kingdom, the kingdom of darkness inside that vessel. I get weary with some people thinking they understand deliverance from demons. We must be careful before Almighty God that we have Kingdom authority before we confront Satan's kingdoms. Some people go through the motions and claim deliverance, but deliverance depends totally upon our confidence in God, knowing who we are and what He has called us to do. Only then can we look with a man's eyes into the spirits of people, way down inside them where unclean spirits are in control, and say, "Unclean spirit, I cast you out by the authority of God that is within me."

Isn't it interesting that a maniac from Capernaum, miles and miles away from Jesus' house, knew exactly who Jesus was? Those who have inner discernment understand that evil spirits know ministries. They know who is on their trail. Satan will allow thousands and thousands of dollars to be available to people who are not bothering his kingdom. But the god of mammon gets angry when he finds one ministry standing on the toes of the devil, saying to Satan, "I'm wise to you. I know who you are and I know what you're all about. I intend to shake and rattle your kingdom." Financial support becomes warfare for a ministry like that. God must awaken the children of the Kingdom to supply the Kingdom's needs. The devil tries to kill, steal and destroy those ministries. But God is going to press the children of the Kingdom into learning how to plant, cultivate, water and reap abundance in Kingdom ministries.

Jesus went to Capernaum to demonstrate His mission—to re-establish Kingdom authority and reclaim the things that were lost in the Garden. Why did Jesus tell His disciples to go to Jerusalem? Jerusalem was the site to begin the final mission of recovery. We know that the sin of the world was Adam and Eve's rebellion against God's plan. God had yet one more plan of recovery through the seed of the woman (Genesis 3:15).

If we fail to understand that our children are essential to God's recovery process and prepare their spirits properly—through sound foundations in scriptural principles and respect for spiritual authority—we make a tragic mistake. Boys and girls must know what has been lost and realize that they are vital in finding and implementing God's plan.

God placed only two standards in the Garden. Everything else was superfluous. One standard was a tree of obedience, the tree of life. God said, "I'm going to make man in My image. I'll put him in a garden on planet earth. I'm going to start with you, Adam. I'm going to tell you about obedience so that you can restore all the earth around about you. By your witness, you will become a prototype that will restore the whole universe."

The second standard God placed in the Garden was the tree of the knowledge of good and evil. Now Adam and Eve had two choices, and the whole plan of God rested on whatever they chose. One was the tree of life, total obedience without wavering. The other choice was the tree of knowledge of good and evil, humanism, doing things "my way." The first plan to defeat satanic forces and recover the universe through obedience failed. Then came the second plan. The tree of the knowledge of good and evil left man outside paradise saying, "I want to know what's right and wrong for myself."

God said, "Okay, I'm going to whip you at your own game, Satan, I'm going to give authority to the seed. Adam, number one, missed the mark. Now I'm going to try it again."

Imagine the choices given to Adam and Eve. On one hand, they could choose the tree of obedience, providing happiness, confidence and the ability to communicate with God and take dominion over the earth.

On the other hand they could choose the tree of the knowledge of good and evil. Eating of this tree would cause them to become their own judges. They wouldn't need anyone to tell them anything. They wouldn't need God, apostles, prophets, evangelists, pastors or teachers. They would be gods unto themselves.

Lucifer tempted Eve, and she chose to eat of the tree of the knowledge of good and evil. When she disobeyed God, she unconsciously moved from the covering of God to the covering of Satan, the god of this world. That position is exactly where the world is today— under Satan's covering.

God's plan of recovering that which was lost through disobedience—simply eating of the tree of obedience— exists in simple little things: living by faith, learning to tithe, forsaking not the assembling of ourselves together, obeying those who are over us in the Lord. The world walks in darkness, waiting to witness the manifestation of the sons of God, waiting for the reality of a new Kingdom.

We must learn to use that heavenly power and authority before the Kingdom can be established. At the Jerusalem happening, God imparted the power to regain happiness, confidence, communication and dominion which were lost in the Garden. Get ready, Church! We have a mission to fulfill!

3

RESTORATION BY THE SEED

After the resurrection Jesus continuously preached the Gospel of the Kingdom. He told His disciples to remain in Jerusalem until they received power from on high (Luke 24:49). His going away was to their advantage because the second phase of God's plan for His Church—the Jerusalem happening—could never occur as long as Jesus was with them (John 16:7).

Then God said, "Let Us make man in Our image, according to Our likeness; let them have dominion over the fish of the sea, over the birds of the air, and over the cattle, over all the earth and over every creeping thing that creeps on the earth." So God created man in His own image; in the image of God He created him; male and female He created them. Then God blessed them, and God said to them, "Be fruitful and multiply; fill the earth and subdue it; have dominion over the fish of the sea, over the birds of the air, and over every living thing that moves on the earth." And God said, "See, I have given you every herb that yields seed which is on the face of all the earth, and every tree whose fruit yields seed; to you it shall be for food. Also, to every beast of the earth, to every bird of the air, and to everything that creeps on the earth, in which there is life, I have given every green herb for food"; and it was so. Then God saw everything that He had made, and indeed it was very good ... (Genesis 1:26-31)

We lost the state of existence that God called "very good." We say to those we love dearly, "I love you very much." We compliment a cook by saying, "My, that was a very good meal." God created an ideal environment which was called "very good" in the midst of a rebellious universe.

"In the beginning God created the heavens and the earth" (Genesis 1:1). Verse two reveals that some disruptive events had already taken place in the universe. The earth was "void and without form." The earth was without order, design, government or purpose. Darkness was on the face of the deep. No light illuminated the planet. The Spirit of God hovered over the face of the earth. Then God said, "Let there be light." Now relate this "light" to Pentecost. Jesus said, "Go to Jerusalem and wait." Just as the Spirit hovered over an earth without form and void, the Spirit also hovered over Jerusalem saying, "A new Kingdom is going to fill the earth."

Pentecost, properly understood, is opening our wills to the Spirit so that He can come in and abide in human flesh. Jesus said, "Go to Jerusalem." But this command can not be separated from the void, dark and futile state of the world we find recorded in Genesis. "That which was lost" began long before the hour God placed man in the garden.

Isaiah records that darkness and confusion disrupted order and design, bringing creation to a void condition. God apparently didn't intend to give us insights into where, when or why this happened, but He did give us some understanding.

"How you are fallen from heaven, O Lucifer, son of the morning! How you are cut down to the ground, you who weakened the nations! For you have said in your heart: 'I will ascend into heaven, I will exalt my throne above the stars of God; I will also sit on the mount of the congregation on the farthest sides of the north; I will ascend above the heights of the clouds, I will be like the Most High.' Yet you shall be brought down to Sheol, to the lowest depths of the Pit. Those who see you will gaze at you, and consider you, saying: 'Is this the man who made the earth tremble, who shook kingdoms, who made the world as a wilderness . . .'" (Isaiah 14:12-16)

When God put a garden in the middle of a wilderness ravaged by satanic forces of rebellion, He was saying, "In this garden I have placed the solution to all problems." God's purpose for creating man was to correct the chaos of the universe. Restoration is the total plan of redemption. God created a paradise as a remedy for devastating rebellion. Understanding God's plan of redemption takes on meaning when we comprehend Jesus' proclamation of His mission on earth.

Two things are important to remember about the Garden: the tree of life represented obedience, and the tree of the knowledge of good and evil represented pride in achievement, or humanism. The humanistic attitude exalts a person as a god unto himself. God used obedience to bring reconciliation to the dark, formless world. If Adam and Eve had partaken obediently of the tree of life, they would have eventually subdued the earth and brought about total correction. But Adam and Eve followed their own desires and ate of the tree of the knowledge of good and evil.

God's second plan for restoration was through the seed of the woman by whom He would eventually bring victory to fallen creation. When we understand God's intentions, we will comprehend the importance of the obedience of Abraham, Isaac, Jacob, the Seed (who is Christ) and Christ's seed (who is the Church).

The story of the battle over the seed is recorded in the twelfth chapter of Revelation. Lucifer understood that the battle was going to be waged between him and the seed of the woman.

Now a great sign appeared in heaven: a woman clothed with the sun, with the moon under her feet, and on her head a garland of twelve stars. Then being with child, she cried out in labor and in pain to give birth. And another sign appeared in heaven: behold, a great, fiery red dragon having seven heads and ten horns, and seven diadems on his heads. His tail drew a third of the stars of heaven and threw them to the earth. And the dragon stood before the woman [Israel, who is a prototype of the Church] *who was ready to give birth, to devour her Child* [who first was Jesus, and then the Church] *as soon as it was born. And she bore a male Child who was to rule all nations with a rod of iron. And her Child was caught up to God and to His throne. Then the woman fled into the wilderness, where she has a place prepared by God . . . And war broke out in heaven: Michael and his angels fought against the dragon; and the dragon and his angels fought, but they did not prevail, nor was a place found for them in heaven any longer. (Revelation 12:1-8)*

Satan is losing his battle in heavenly places as he wages war primarily on the earth. If the Church is to withstand the forces of the devil over the seed, she must move with tremendous authority and power.

So the great dragon was cast out, that serpent of old, called the Devil and Satan, who deceives the whole world; he was cast to the earth, and his angels were cast out with him. Then I heard a loud voice saying in heaven, "Now salvation, and strength, and the kingdom of our God, and the power of His Christ have come, for the accuser of our brethren, who accused them before our God day and night, has been cast down. And they overcame him by the blood of the Lamb and by the word of their testimony, and they did not love their lives to the death. Therefore rejoice, O heavens, and you who dwell in them! Woe to the inhabitants of the earth and the sea! For the devil has come down to you, having great wrath, because he knows that he has a short time." (Revelation 12:9-12)

Satan is no longer alive and well. He has been mortally wounded. Although he thinks he may come to life again, his time is short. A foot rests on his neck. Praise God, he will not prevail!

Now when the dragon saw that he had been cast to the earth, he persecuted the woman who gave birth to the male Child. But the woman was given two wings of a great eagle, that she might fly into the wilderness to her place, where she is nourished for a time and times and half a time, from the presence of the serpent. So the serpent spewed water out of his mouth like a flood after the woman, that he might cause her to be carried away by the flood. But the earth helped the woman, and the earth opened its mouth and swallowed up the flood which the dragon had spewed out of his mouth. And the dragon was enraged with the woman, and he went to make war with the rest of her offspring, who keep the commandments of God and have the testimony of Jesus Christ. (Revelation 12:13-17)

We are now living out God's second plan to redeem "that which was lost." The predominant themes of the Bible are regaining what was lost, the strategy to regain creation, and the importance of the seed who will bring about the fulfillment of God's plan. We must dedicate our lives to the strategy that God gives us.

The consequences that we face because of man's disobedience are recorded in Genesis 3. These judgments are extremely important for us to understand in our spirits in order to press toward restoration.

So the Lord God said to the serpent: "Because you have done this, you are cursed more than all cattle, and more than every beast of the field; on your belly you shall go, and you shall eat dust all the days of your life. And I will put enmity between you and the woman, and between your seed and her Seed; He shall bruise your head, and you shall bruise His heel." To the woman He said: "I will greatly multiply your sorrow and your conception; in pain you shall bring forth children; your desire shall be for your husband, and he shall rule over you." Then to Adam He said, "*Because you have heeded the voice of your wife, and have eaten from the tree of which I commanded you, saying, 'You shall not eat of it': Cursed is the ground for your sake; in toil you shall eat of it all the days of your life. Both thorns and thistles it shall bring forth for you, and you shall eat the herb of the field. In the sweat of your face you shall eat bread till you return to the ground, for out of it you were taken. For dust you are, and to dust you shall return.*" (Genesis 3:14-19)

Jesus Christ came to break the curse over mankind. "Christ has redeemed us from the curse of the law, having become a curse for us (for it is written, 'Cursed is everyone who hangs on a tree')" (Galatians 3:13). That curse is broken in us by the Kingdom of God. The degree to which we live out our freedom is the degree to which we comprehend faith at work today. God said to the serpent, "I am going to place enmity between your seed and her seed. You will bruise the heel of the seed of the woman, but you won't be able to get to her head. However, her Seed is going to crush your head."

God told Eve that she would bring forth the seed in pain. The Bible declares, "A child left to himself brings shame to his mother," not to his father. Pain is an ingredient of motherhood, not just in physical birth, but throughout a child's lifetime. To Adam He said, "The ground is cursed. Creation is no longer under your command."

Warfare rages everywhere today—kingdom against kingdom—seed against seed—nation against nation.

Wars erupt in the heavenlies, and wars tell the story of human history—Germany, Korea, Viet Nam. Wars and rumors of wars are caused by the consequences of our evil.

A battle is raging over our seed. A far greater problem exists in interrupting pregnancy than simply the social issue of abortion. The root issue is that Satan wants to kill the seed. He will kill thousands of babies to get to one Kingdom baby. When Jesus Christ was born, Herod commanded his soldiers to kill children by the thousands. Whom did he really want to destroy? He was targeting only one Seed. Thousands of babies are destroyed in abortion clinics because Satan wants to stop the principle of multiplying spiritual children. He who has ears to hear, let him hear what the Spirit is saying!

Satan attacks the seed through social lifestyles. The great problem that homosexual or lesbian communities pose to God's plan is not only that lifestyle, but also Satan wants to pervert man's desires so that no seed will be produced. If Satan can make men effeminate and women masculine, he will effectively destroy the seed principle. Satan's real victory comes when he perverts our natural desires.

A major problem in the Church today concerns religious activities exclusively for men or strictly for women. Dangers emerge when women work in spiritual ministries without spiritual input from a man. Likewise, men who proceed in the ministry without the spiritual input of women are quickly in danger of inadequate discernment. God made man, male and

50

female, and blessed them in that relationship.

This male/female concept must be spiritually implemented for the full counsel of ministry in the Church. God said, "I will pour out my Spirit in the last days upon sons and daughters." The problems in the Church cannot be solved if Satan can divide total counsel in ministries. The division of men and women in ministry is a subtle way by which Satan will try to destroy spiritual seed. Both male and female are required to create a physical offspring, and they are both required to produce the spiritual seed that will defeat Satan.

The Church should be careful not to have gatherings that are exclusive: all women, or all men, or conferences of some type—just "clerical collar" wearers, for example. We are all one in Christ.

The real battle in education is over the seed principle. Satan attacks public education by going against the principle of raising boys and girls according to the admonition of God's Word. Honoring parents and understanding authority are biblical principles that must be taught if our children are to fulfill their destiny as the seed of Jesus Christ. God moved in my spirit to begin an educational program in our church because I am totally convinced in my heart that God must raise up examples, prototypes, that will challenge the failures of humanistic, public education. A standard must be demonstrated because God judges the world by standards.

The famine in Ethiopia is the result of man losing

control of the earth. What did God say to Adam? "The earth will fail to yield its fruit." Pollution in the water and air also shows that man has lost his authority on the earth. I believe that God will show us that even today we can begin to restore ecological balance. We must regain command of the earth and the circumstances in which we live. Until we do, Christ cannot return.

A "waiting" bride and a "preparing" bride are not the same kind of woman. A bride who sits around waiting or sleeping until her wedding day is unlike the bride who prepares diligently for her groom. The foolish virgins failed to prepare themselves while the wise virgins waited aggressively, preparing their lamps. God will only use young men and women who have prepared themselves. That preparation must go beyond academic education. The "preparing" bride must aggressively search God's Word and be sensitive to spiritual insights so that God can say, "I trust her spirit."

A person who is anxious for natural relationships can solve that anxiety by reaching his potential as a follower and minister of Jesus Christ. God will bring satisfying relationships into a person's life if he sets the Kingdom as the top priority. If one searches and frets over natural needs, he will likely become involved in wrong relationships and create terrible personal problems.

God's "Plan B" is the strategy by which the seed will overcome Satan's rule. The earth is the Lord's and the fullness thereof, but Satan's system dominates man's thinking today. Satan took Jesus to the mountaintop and said, "Look at all this. I have dominion and authority over it," but Jesus answered, "I have come to seek and to save that which was lost." What was lost? The rule of the earth. The power over the seed. We must regain everything that was lost. Jesus Christ began reclaiming creation when He was on the earth, and we now continue His mission. His Body will completely reclaim what was lost as a witness to the world.

That message of action shakes and rattles people. Many people who accept Jesus Christ sit back saying, "Oh, come, Lord Jesus! Come, Lord Jesus! Let other people starve to death. Let people in educational systems tend to their own worries. I am just going to sit here and wait for Jesus to come back." Jesus will never come to a lazy bride who is not pressing, proclaiming and preparing herself for the coming of her bridegroom.

Since the fall of man in the Garden, God has looked for someone who would establish a principle on which He could have an overcoming seed. Finally, God found Abram.

God said, "Abram, leave your country, your kindred and your father's house. Go to a land that I will show you" (Genesis 12:1). God wasn't interested in moving Abram's household. God wanted one thing from Abram—obedience. How many other people God called besides Abram, nobody will ever know. He could have called thousands, but Abram was the first to respond to God's call. He left his country without knowing where he was going out of absolute and total obedience to

God's voice. Some people don't believe in blind obedience. What other kind of obedience is there? "Seeing"
obedience contradicts faith. When Abram said "yes,"
the Lord probably turned to His angels, Michael and
Gabriel, and said, "Perhaps we have found our man."

God is looking for obedience and faith by which we
will overcome the world (I John 5:4). Abraham and
Sarah were too old to produce a seed except through a
miracle. Abraham had faith that God would make provisions for him because he lived by the faith principle.
The Bible clearly says, "In Isaac, my promise was
made." God made a promise to Abraham, but in Isaac
the promise was realized. Why Isaac? Because Isaac
was a miracle child, conceived beyond natural ability.
The promise was given by God to Abraham that all the
earth would be blessed through his seed Isaac.

"But it is not that the word of God has taken no effect.
For they are not all Israel who are of Israel, nor are they
all children because they are the seed of Abraham; but,
'In Isaac your seed shall be called' " (Romans 9:6-7).
Many people never comprehend the meaning of that
passage. They say they are "the seed" because they are
sons of Abraham. You can be a seed of Abraham and
still not belong to the household of promise. "In Isaac
your seed shall be called" through a miracle birth.

*By faith Abraham, when he was tested, offered up Isaac,
and he who had received the promises offered up his only
begotten son, of whom it was said, "In Isaac your seed
shall be called," accounting that God was able to raise
him up, even from the dead, from which he also received
him in a figurative sense. (Hebrews 11:17-19)*

Incidents in the Word of the Lord must be understood as shadows, types and figurative examples. Through His promise, God allowed the birth of Isaac even though Abraham and Sarah were sexually dead. Even though God required Abraham to offer Isaac as a sacrifice, Abraham still believed God's promise because he was a man of faith.

A concept that delights me is "the fruit of innocence." The Bible says, "Whoever does not receive the kingdom of God as a little child will by no means enter it"(Luke 18:17). Innocence! That word implies absolute obedience. A two-year-old child who loves and trusts his parents will jump into their arms from a high place. What would happen if someone tried that test with a twenty-five-year-old woman or a forty-year-old man? They would say, "Now hold it just a minute. Do you have some extra support down there? Do you have someone else to help you catch me?"

When we understand obedience in faith, we are ready to implement "overcoming by the blood of the Lamb, by the word of our testimony, and by loving not our lives unto death." Overcoming to that degree demands total obedience. Through suffering, Jesus Christ became obedient. In Christ's suffering, God gave Him authority. Jesus was the sacrificed Lamb of God, making provision for His sheep to overcome in the Spirit of the Lamb. Sheep living in the spirit of the Lamb can overcome just as Jesus did.

Where does Moses fit into God's plan? Moses' mission was one of correction, but the law never brings people to redemption. Paul explained to the Galatian church the difference between the covenant of the law and the covenant that is in Jesus Christ, the One who is descended from Isaac. The Galatians wanted to go back to the law:

> *Tell me, you who desire to be under the law, do you not hear the law? For it is written that Abraham had two sons: the one by a bondwoman, the other by a freewoman. But he who was of the bondwoman was born according to the flesh, and he of the freewoman through promise, which things are symbolic. For these are the two covenants: the one from Mount Sinai which gives birth to bondage, which is Hagar—for this Hagar is Mount Sinai in Arabia, and corresponds to Jerusalem which now is, and is in bondage with her children—but the Jerusalem above is free, which is the mother of us all. For it is written: "Rejoice, O barren, you who do not bear! Break forth and shout, you who do not travail! For the desolate has many more children than she who has a husband." Now we, brethren, as Isaac was, are children of promise. But, as he who was born according to the flesh then persecuted him who was born according to the Spirit, even so it is now . . . "Cast out the bondwoman and her son, for the son of the bondwoman shall not be heir with the son of the freewoman." So then, brethren, we are not children of the bondwoman but of the free. (Galatians 4:21-31)*

The law was given to inform people about sin. The people cried to Moses and their behavior indicated, "We don't know what sin is." God instructed Moses to give them the law. God took his prophet to the mountain to give him a revelation about the Kingdom, but first He had to give him a revelation about the law. Paul said,

"The law is a school master," and the law has nothing to offer the seed except to correct behavior. Paul wrote, "What purpose then does the law serve?" (Galatians 3:19). The law was added after Abraham. "Because of transgression," God gave the law. If people were obedient to God, the law would have been totally unnecessary.

Why must God impose laws on people today? God must require a tithe of our income because of spiritual transgression. If people gave according to faith, that law would be needless. Jesus said, "You are going to tithe or I am not going to bless you." Paul said that the law would be unnecessary if we understood that we were to give as the Lord prospers us. Many people still do not understand the principle that God requires ten percent of a believer's income.

The law ruled God's people in an intermediate period of history. God said to Abraham, "I am going to give you seed." God gave the law to Abraham's seed through Moses. The law was given because of transgression until the promised Seed came to fulfill it. I believe if Abraham's descendants had understood God's promises and acted on them, Jesus Christ would have come in the flesh earlier in history. Because of the disobedience in many hearts and minds, Christ waits even now to establish His Kingdom on earth.

Jesus Christ waits to come again because of a lack of obedience and faith. He is literally waiting in the heavens until He finds "a people." Why should we force Him to wait any longer? When He finds "a people who were not a people," God can say that righteousness has prevailed and Christ can come again. Oh, I would love for Jesus to come in the next few years! Wouldn't that be wonderful? Impossible? I don't believe so. But we can't just sit back, look up, watch, wait and sing, "I'll Fly Away." Never! Never! On the authority of God's Word, I promise that attitude won't work! Instead we must say, "God, the seed principle is obedience and faith. We are going to learn how to move in faith. We want to learn how to move in obedience." Paul said, "Now to Abraham and his Seed were the promises made. He does not say, 'And to seeds,' as of many, but as of one" (Galatians 3:16). Understand that principle by the Spirit. Recognize the importance of knowing that the seed is Jesus Christ. It is not many seeds; it is one Seed, Jesus Christ.

Jesus told His disciples, "I want you to remain in Jerusalem to be empowered to complete My work." We are about to move into a second phase of understanding the mission of the Church because we have established that Jesus Christ is "the Seed."

Most assuredly, I say to you, he who believes in Me, the works that I do he will do also; and greater works than these he will do, because I go to My Father. And whatever you ask in My name, that I will do, that the Father may be glorified in the Son. If you ask anything in My name, I will do it. If you love Me, keep My commandments. And I will pray the Father, and He will give you another Helper, that He will abide with you forever, even the Spirit of truth, whom the world cannot receive, because it neither sees Him nor knows Him; but you know Him, for He dwells with you and will be in you. I will not leave you orphans; I will come to you. (John 14:12-18)

"I will not leave you orphans." Pentecost is all about His helping us to complete a mission on earth. Without the Holy Spirit in us, we are orphans. Many churches today are orphanages. No orphans are found wherever the Holy Spirit dwells. People dance and rejoice when called leadership covers them and the enduement of the Holy Spirit gives them power. The fires of Pentecost burn in those churches.

These things I have spoken to you while being present with you. But the Helper, the Holy Spirit, whom the Father will send in My name, He will teach you all things, and bring to your remembrance all things that I said to you. Peace I leave with you, My peace I give to you; not as the world gives do I give to you. Let not your heart be troubled, neither let it be afraid. You have heard Me say to you, "I am going away and coming back to you." If you loved Me, you would rejoice because I said, "I am going to the Father," for My Father is greater than I. And now I have told you before it comes, that when it does come to pass, you may believe. I will no longer talk much with you, for the ruler of this world is coming, and he has nothing in Me. (John 14:25-30)

Where is our warfare today? We war against the ruler of this world. Jesus met him on the mount of temptation. The Church will also meet him on the mount of temptation. This is God's hour of proving His Church.

But now I go away to Him who sent Me, and none of you asks Me, "Where are You going?" But because I have said these things to you, sorrow has filled your heart. Nevertheless I tell you the truth. It is to your advantage that I go away; for if I do not go away, the Helper will not come to

*you; but if I depart, I will send Him to you. And when He
has come, He will convict the world of sin, and of righteousness, and of judgment. (John 16:5-8)*

What happened at Jerusalem will convict the world
of sin. God's Church, building the standard of righteousness, proclaiming the witness of Christ, will convict the world of sin. God must find a standard by
which He can judge the world.

An accurate measurement of three feet requires a
yardstick. The Church is to be God's "yardstick" to
judge the world. God can never judge the world until a
mature Church is His "yardstick." God must be able to
say to the world, "You have seen my mature Church.
She is a standard." That demonstration is the witness
principle. Jesus' commission is, "Go into all the world
and preach the gospel—establish a standard by your
witness wherever you go."

*There is neither Jew nor Greek, there is neither slave nor
free, there is neither male nor female; for you are all one in
Christ Jesus. And if you are Christ's, then you are Abraham's seed, and heirs according to the promise. (Galatians 3:28-29)*

Abraham's seed is Christ and His Church. If we are
the seed of Jesus Christ and heirs according to the
promise, then we are the seed of Abraham. This heritage means that we are of Christ, the seed of God Himself. We need to understand that we are sons of God. We
must be recognized as being His sons and daughters by
the world. The completion of the incarnation of God in
the world must be in His Church. The Church must

understand that she, too, is the seed of Abraham. Jesus Christ is the firstfruit, but without the ongoing harvest, the incarnation will never be complete.

Jesus Christ is the standard of the total incarnation of God as far as individual believers are concerned. An ongoing incarnation in the corporate Church is necessary for the seed to prevail against disobedience.

The Church will win the ancient battle between the seed of the woman and the seed of the serpent. We are the seed of Abraham. We are going to overcome the devil through Jesus' gift to us at Pentecost. The two weapons used to overcome the devil are faith and obedience.

Jesus said, "I will build My church, and the gates of Hades [hell] shall not prevail against it" (Matthew 16:18). He said that He would give us authority to loose and bind (verse 19). Until the Church exercises her authority, Jesus Christ will never return. Until the Church knows who she is, she cannot rule as the bride of Christ. The Church is like an immature teenager, running around, confused, searching for purpose.

The bride who is preparing for her wedding has her hope chest filled, her lamps trimmed and burning, and she lacks nothing. She has a keen mind, a discerner of spirits. She knows her calling and she stands ready to meet any challenge. When she makes world systems His footstool, she stands up and says, "Come, Lord Jesus! All things are made ready!" The Son of Man will split the sky in power, great authority and glory. He will come for His bride. We will rejoice at the exciting marriage supper of the Lamb. We will see God's Kingdom, totally restored, just like it was at the very beginning.

Circumcision of heart through water baptism moves us from the kingdom of darkness to the Kingdom of light. God must be weary of people being baptized without understanding His covenant. They are immersed a dry sinner and brought up a wet sinner— never knowing what baptism means. Many people talk about baptism being "an outward sign of an inward grace." That phraseology is not in the Bible. Water baptism is being "buried with Christ." We no longer live as a part of "Hagar's seed principle" which is ruled by the mind of reason. We now live as children of faith and obedience, walking in the seed principle of God's promise.

Jesus said, "I will pour out of My Spirit on all flesh; your sons and your daughters [the spiritual seed] shall prophesy" (Acts 2:17). The seed are to be baptized and brought alive with new enlightenment. Pentecost, the day of the outpouring of the Holy Spirit, was the beginning of the end for the devil. God's authority was brought alive in His Church.

The church at Laodicea heard these words, "Because you say, 'I am rich, have become wealthy, and have need of nothing'—and do not know that you are wretched, miserable, poor, blind and naked . . ." (Revelation 3:17). We are in the Laodicean period in terms of the sequence of history.

The Laodicean Church was blind and naked. "I counsel you to buy from Me gold refined in the fire, that you may be rich; and white garments, that you may be clothed, that the shame of your nakedness may not be revealed; and anoint your eyes with eye salve, that you may see" (Revelation 3:18). We are approaching a time and place when God, through the witness principle and the fruit of innocence, will clothe us in His righteousness.

True holiness is being clothed in His righteousness. God is finding His Church—those who know they are the seed of Abraham. They are the promise of Isaac's birth. They are seed unto Christ. As that seed, they are beginning to move in His righteousness.

How do we regain the confidence and innocence that were lost in the Garden? We must be clothed in His righteousness, which gives us confidence. We are no longer naked. We can defeat the devil because we are washed in the blood of the Lamb. We can resist his accusations. We have been been baptized, "circumcision of the heart." We can live confidently in His Kingdom when we realize that we are children of the King. Even when we make mistakes, we won't wallow in our sins. We will repent and receive restoration.

But if we walk in the light as He is in the light, we have fellowship with one another, and the blood of Jesus Christ His Son cleanses us from all sin. (I John 1:7)

If we confess our sins, He is faithful and just to forgive us our sins, and to cleanse us from all unrighteousness. (I John 1:9)

63

We have the answers to problems, but those answers require obedience and faith. We cannot refuse to take communion, be baptized, commit ourselves to a church fellowship, or have eldership over us in the Lord. Our maturity is dependent upon absolute faith and obedience. The world is full of people who are their own gods. They have chosen the tree of the knowledge of good and evil. God is looking for those who choose the tree of life. These people become the seed of obedience and faith. They are Abraham's seed who will complete God's plan of restoration.

4

EXPERIENCE IN THE UPPER ROOM

The disciples had the scriptures, but it took Jesus' demonstration of truth to open their understanding. Today many people perceive the Bible as a book of history or poetry, but they don't understand it as a book of revelation becoming reality in the world today. Our understanding of scripture must be opened by the Holy Spirit.

Then He said to them, "Thus it is written, and thus it was necessary for the Christ to suffer and to rise from the dead the third day, and that repentance and remission of sins should be preached in His name to all nations, beginning at Jerusalem. And you are witnesses of these things. Behold, I send the Promise of My Father upon you; but tarry in the city of Jerusalem until you are endued with power from on high." (Luke 24:46-49)

Jesus had given the promise that the Holy Spirit would come. Now He was giving his disciples specific directions. They were to tarry in Jerusalem in prayer. His purpose for having them together was so that they might enter into an atmosphere of expectancy. They also had to reach a place of total unity so that Christ could come among them through the power of the Holy Spirit.

The former account I made, O Theophilus, of all that Jesus began both to do and teach, until the day in which He was taken up, after He through the Holy Spirit had given commandments to the apostles whom He had chosen, to whom He also presented Himself alive after His suffering by many infallible proofs, being seen by them during forty days and speaking of the things pertaining to the kingdom of God. And being assembled together with them, He commanded them not to depart from Jerusalem, but to wait for the Promise of the Father, "which," He said, "you have heard from Me; for John truly baptized with water, but you shall be baptized with the Holy Spirit not many days from now." Therefore, when they had come together, they asked Him, saying, "Lord, will You at this time restore the kingdom to Israel?" (Acts 1:1-6)

Everything Jesus taught His disciples for forty days after His resurrection was about the Kingdom. Their question was, "Is this the beginning of the Kingdom rule? Is this the beginning of Your promise to us? Is this the beginning of Your reign?" Jesus answered, "It is not for you to know times or seasons which the Father has put in His own authority." In response to the disciples' questions, He continued, "But you shall receive power when the Holy Spirit has come upon you; and you shall be witnesses to Me in Jerusalem, and in all Judea and Samaria, and to the end of the earth."

Then they returned to Jerusalem from the Mount called Olivet, which is near Jerusalem, a Sabbath day's journey. And when they had entered, they went up into the upper room where they were staying: Peter, James, John, and Andrew; Philip and Thomas; Bartholomew and Matthew; James the son of Alphaeus and Simon the Zealot; and Judas the son of James. These all continued with one accord in prayer and supplication, with the women and Mary the mother of Jesus, and with His brothers. And in those days Peter stood up in the midst of the disciples (altogether the number of names was about a hundred and twenty), and said, "Men and brethren, this Scripture had to be fulfilled, which the Holy Spirit spoke before by the mouth of David concerning Judas, who became a guide to those who arrested Jesus; for he was numbered with us and obtained a part in this ministry." (Now this man purchased a field with the wages of iniquity; and falling headlong, he burst open in the middle and all his entrails gushed out. And it became known to all those dwelling in Jerusalem; so that field is called in their own language, Akel Dama, that is, Field of Blood.) "For it is written in the book of Psalms: 'Let his habitation be desolate, and let no one live in it'; and, 'Let another take his office.' Therefore, of these men who have accompanied us all the time that the Lord Jesus went in and out among us, beginning from the baptism of John to that day when He was taken up from us, one of these must become a witness with us of His resurrection." And they proposed two: Joseph called Barsabas, who was surnamed Justus, and Matthias. And they prayed and said, "You, O Lord, who know the hearts of all, show which of these two You have chosen to take part in this ministry and apostleship from which Judas by transgression fell, that he might go to his own place." And they cast their lots, and the lot fell on Matthias. And he was numbered with the eleven apostles. (Acts 1:12-26)

"Now when the Day of Pentecost had fully come, they were all in one place in one accord." I do not believe that the disciples went into the upper room in one accord. I believe they came into unity while they were there. Many matters had to be settled among them. Finally, they were able to come into unity so that God could release the Holy Spirit.

The number, one hundred and twenty, is symbolic. The figure twelve (the trinity involved with the four corners of the earth) and the zero behind it represents an extension of God's involvement in the earth. Ten is the number of perfection. The number represents a larger dimension of God's manifestation in the earth. The disciples in the upper room only represented many people of God to come. The one hundred and twenty represented a prototype of many groups of believers who would gather in one accord. Likewise, the two witnesses are a prototype of the dual witness of the Church. Every aspect of this important event has a meaning. God chose twelve disciples (God in the earth). God gave mankind ten commandments (a complete number to perfect them). These numbers are not meaningless. God gave order and design so that we might have a shadow or a type to understand His ways.

Just as Jesus is the firstfruit of many brethren, Pentecost is a firstfruit of events in the latter reign of God in His Church. Knowing that, we must examine the disciples' circumstances, battles, defeats and victories.

Neither the cross nor the resurrection was the culmination of Jesus Christ's ministry. The cross teaches us the necessity of sacrificing our wills. The resurrection teaches us the reward of God's power at work in us. Pentecost is the culmination of the ministry of Jesus Christ. Pentecost is the culmination of the total revelation God began speaking to man in Genesis. Every intention of God at Pentecost is inseparable from God's purposes in Genesis.

The baptism of the Holy Spirit is not just an emotional experience—it is an enduement of authority to accomplish God's purposes on planet Earth. The Holy Spirit came to insure that God's intentions are fulfilled in His people. The Holy Spirit once moved on the waters when the earth was void and formless. Now the Holy Spirit moves upon a company of people to release God's power to restore the earth, to restore the Kingdom. The theme of Pentecost is restoration.

The Spirit of Christ had to be transferred to the disciples. Jesus led His disciples to Bethany and He blessed them (Luke 24:50). I believe that His blessing began the transfer of His Spirit. The gift of the Holy Spirit at Pentecost brings the Spirit of Christ within us. That gift ignites God's Kingdom of righteousness, peace and joy within us and moves us to action. That gift triggers implementation of the Kingdom. After we experience Pentecost, we become "Christ" to the world. The Man,

Jesus Christ, is no longer here in the flesh. Jesus said, "It is expedient that I go away so the Holy Spirit will come."

"However, when He, the Spirit of truth, has come, He will guide you into all truth; for He will not speak on His own authority, but whatever He hears He will speak; and He will tell you things to come" (John 16:13). We become temples of the Holy Spirit. Christ takes up residence within us. The Spirit of Christ was transferred into one hundred and twenty people at Pentecost. They became "Christ" to the world.

Somewhere along the way, the Church has lost that understanding. We became self-centered, believing the Holy Spirit came to give us good feelings, good experiences, security and access to personal guidance. Indeed, the Holy Spirit grants us all those things, but the purpose of the Holy Spirit is to give us the authority to bring God's will to pass upon this planet. Some vital ingredients are necessary to accomplish God's intentions:

First of all, God must have a united people. God's desire since Adam and Eve has been to have a people with whom He could interact. This desire in God's heart cannot be separated from Pentecost. God wants a people who are united against chaos, disorder and formless voids in creation. God's will brings purpose and design. Harmony and unity are God's intentions. Pentecost is the answer to disillusionment, to any destruction of the universe. Order, purpose, design—all come about through God's people united in His Spirit.

God ordains fixed principles in His creation. God said, "It is not good that man should be alone." Note that nothing is said about God walking "in the garden in the cool of the day" until He had two to walk with Him. God is one, but it takes two to find Him. Someone asks, "Can I never find Him alone?" A person will never walk in God's purposes alone. Christians must always be in fellowship. Jesus said, "Where two or three are agreed." God wants a people in unity. He starts with a very basic prototype in unity. He says, "Give me two or three in agreement. I will expand their unity to one hundred and twenty people, and then expand their unity to the universal Church."

Pentecost is the Spirit of unity. When we understand unity, we comprehend the heart of Pentecost, "what God joins together." Pentecost is joining spirits together in Christ. Though Judas was physically one of the disciples, he never united with the others in spirit. Finally, Judas' separation was lived out through betrayal in the flesh.

Until God can find a people in unity of faith and spirit, Jesus Christ will never return. Someone asks, "Then you do not believe in the imminent return of Jesus Christ?" I believe in the return of Jesus Christ when God's requirements are met. We are playing games by believing that God is going to surprise His people. We are the children of light! We will know the season of His coming! That season requires unity of faith. The whole purpose for apostles, prophets, evangelists, pastors and teachers is to bring the Body into unity of faith! God said to me, "Give Me an Operation of Unity in the Church and I will give you Christ." He will never come until we implement God's will according to His Word.

"That they all may be one, as You are in Me, and I in You; that the world may believe that You sent Me" (John 17:21). Our mission is to let the world know, give them a standard, a witness, a demonstration of truth and light by which they can be judged.

The second ingredient in accomplishing God's intentions is a transfer of God's Spirit. "But if the Spirit of Him who raised Jesus from the dead dwells in you, He who raised Christ from the dead will also give life to your mortal bodies through His Spirit who dwells in you" (Romans 8:11). The Spirit of God dwelling in us is the essence of Pentecost. Pentecost endued a united body with power from on high.

When Ezekiel saw the revelation of the Church in the last days, he saw bones lying here and bones lying there. God told the prophet, "Prophesy over them!" God is raising up men and women today to prophesy over the scattered bones of His Body. Pentecostal power unites a disjointed body, bringing it together by the Spirit. As long as a body is fragmented, no life exists.

Ministries of restoration are being raised up today in power and authority. God has called these ministries to prophesy over the dry bones of the Church and bring them to life. The outpouring of the Holy Spirit will soon flood the world. We have only had a taste of the outpouring of the Spirit. Spiritual unity, at a measure like the world has never known, will become such a powerful witness that powers and principalities of darkness will stand back fearful and helpless at what they see taking place.

The one hundred and twenty had an injection of God's Spirit in the upper room. God transferred His Spirit into them. They heard the sound of a mighty rushing wind; they saw tongues of fire sitting upon each of them; they heard the manifestation of God's presence and power. But that wonderful experience was like a dam holding water. The full release of the Spirit came when they rushed down into the streets. They immediately started implementing the authority they had received. The world does not need a Church secluded in the upper room. The world needs us in the streets—living, demonstrating the Gospel of the Kingdom.

Look at the results of taking God's authority to the streets. "Then those who gladly received His word were baptized; and that day about three thousand souls were added to them" (Acts 2:41). The result of unity was Pentecost. The result of Pentecost was the enduement of power. The enduement of power brought the release of the Spirit of God to the world resulting in converted souls. Only this sequence demonstrates true Pentecost. "And they continued steadfastly in the apostles' doctrine and fellowship, in the breaking of bread, and in prayers." They continued under God's ordained spiritual headship.

One of the greatest problems in the Church today is Christians' unwillingness to continue under spiritual headship's authority. The early Christians continued with the apostles—where God's anointing flowed decently and in order. "Then fear came upon every soul, and many wonders and signs were done through the apostles." Why? Because Pentecost was reality. Through a oneness in Spirit, God could release His power at the hands of the apostles.

"Now all who believed were together." A believing, unified group is unstoppable. We have many believers in the Church today, but not unity of Spirit. Pentecost demonstrated many believers in one accord. "Now all who believed were together, and had all things in common." The Church is a Body that does not belong to itself. The head cannot say to the hand, "I have no need of you," nor can the foot say to the arm, "I have no need of you." Until we realize a oneness, the authority of God will never be poured out in this world. As long as we are concerned about our own kingdoms and our own welfare, Jesus Christ will never return. The Holy Spirit did not come until God's people were in unity and Jesus Christ will not break the character of the Holy Spirit.

Those who had been filled with the Spirit of God continued in unity. They went from house to house for fellowship. They were a people of joy (Acts 2:46). Christians no longer were in one place, but they remained in one accord. A body of believers must be united in one Spirit. When people are in one Spirit in unity, love abounds. Out of that Spirit, numerical growth in the Church is inevitable. In that unity, miracles become everyday blessings.

Peter and John went to the temple to pray. A man, lame from his mother's womb, lay at the gate of the temple asking alms from those who entered. Many passed the man, probably giving him monetary gifts. But when he asked Peter and John for alms, they simply looked into his eyes and said, "Look at us." The man probably thought he was going to get a good offering from them. Peter and John, in unity of Spirit, gave him something that natural man could never give him. The apostles gave the man a visitation of the Spirit of God. Why? Peter and John were in one accord. They had authority with God. The world sits at the doorstep of the Church asking, "Who is your God? Can He help me?" They don't care about our doctrines or labels. The "lame" of the world just want to know whether God is real in Christians who call themselves "God's people."

When the Lord spoke to my heart about "Operation Unity," I began to see by the Spirit so many things that had gone unnoticed—things that seemed so obvious. The core of the matter is that we are not aware of God's heart. We concentrate on matters affecting us while God stands back saying, "Wake up, children! Wake up! I have put you on the earth to show the world something!"

I watched my niece, Deanna, literally play with her mother one afternoon in the hospital shortly before Joan's death. I watched her as she took Joan's limp arms and put them around her neck. I saw her baby her mother's face. Deanna gave her mother commands in the Spirit. Joan puckered her lips and kissed her daughter in a playful mood. I sat there absolutely overcome with wonder, and yet I saw a spiritual demonstration that is so real. The flesh itself—even in physical weakness—is responsive to the Spirit.

Several days later, Joan's body was unresponsive, seeming to have no life at all. Bishop Harry Mushegan, Pastor Sam Lalaian and I started singing and praising the Lord. We watched Joan's feeble hand as she tried to lift it in praise to God. Later, our family gathered in Joan's room to sing and pray. We began to see the spirit come alive in Joan. We prayed with such unity that in the midst of that worship Joan revived so that I could communicate with her. I said to her, "Honey, do you know where you are? Do you know what is taking place?" Joan answered, "Yes, I know Jesus!" I asked her, "Do you see Jesus?" Oh, yes, she did! Just as surely as Stephen saw Jesus standing at the right hand of the Father, Joan saw into that sphere, too.

Powers move all around us. They fight intense warfare over us. They battle for the minds of our boys and girls. They battle over our spirits. Warfare rages in the heavenlies and we, God's people, must be sensitive to it. We become witnesses to the principalities and powers in heavenly places (Ephesians 3:10). The Church endures the attack from every power of darkness in the universe while the devil points an accusing finger at us saying, "They'll never pull it off!" But Jesus, the Lion of Judah, says, "God, give them time! They're going to do it!"

When warfare erupts within the ranks of the Church, God says to the devil, "Hold it! Have you seen that little church on the side of a hill in North Carolina who are in one accord? Have you seen that little group of people meeting in that little hut in an African village?" The problem has been that the bones have been separated all over the world. God is saying to His prophets by the Spirit, "Prophesy!" Join groups together—not by organization—but by a spiritual oneness. When the world observes one Church speaking one voice, they will know our common denominator is the witness of Jesus Christ. In that witness, God can shatter the forces of world systems. The Kingdom comes no other way.

When God's people came into unity in the upper room, the Holy Spirit fell. Then God began to assign various tasks for people to do. He said to Peter in a vision, "I want you to minister to the Gentiles." Peter was a Jew who didn't like the Gentiles. God spoke to Him concerning prejudices between Gentiles and Jews. "What God has cleansed you must not call common" (Acts 10:15). Peter had just seen the vision from God when he heard a knock at the door. Nothing happens accidentally in God's will. Even as the men were inquiring about Peter's whereabouts, God spoke to Him saying, "Behold, three men are seeking you." Immediately the spiritual vision was lived out in Peter's emotions. Obedience in this situation was probably still very difficult for Peter, but he swallowed his pride and obeyed God.

Ministries are dying because they fail to broaden their umbrella of covering. God has provided certain ministries with television equipment and satellite opportunities to bring far-reaching unity to the family of God. If these ministries close off other ministries who may not be in total agreement with them, I prophesy that people doing the cutting will not only falter and fail, they will lose their opportunities to minister.

We must be sure the umbrella is broad enough to receive all of God's children. "Red and yellow, black and white, they are precious in His sight." We sit around deciding by our own rules and regulations "who will do what." God says, "Hold it! I've made you one blood, one family, one calling. Be sure you include everybody whom I approve!" All people, all things were created for the glory and honor of God.

Paul was a highly educated, devout Jew who was knowledgeable in the Jewish law. Because of his sincere zeal, he sought and persecuted those who had experienced Christ and the "Jerusalem Happening." Through a miraculous encounter with Jesus, Paul's eyes were opened and he became a unifying force between the Jews and Gentiles.

James was called to be a bishop, probably the first in the Church. When problems arose concerning circumcision, the apostles and elders met together. James sat quietly listening to their debates. When they finished arguing, James began to speak. He made the final decision of what they should do. He was called by God to be the one to reconcile conflicting situations and opinions. When God places a man in the office of a bishop, He gives that servant spiritual wisdom to handle conflicts in the ministry.

Everything was going great for the early Church. They were having a wonderful time serving the Lord and enjoying the new fellowship of the Holy Spirit. People were being healed. Those owning land and possessions sold them and gave the money to the apostles to distribute. No one lacked provisions among the people. Everything was glorious! Then something went wrong.

First, they started loving money more than God. Ananias and Sapphira were the first to break the covenant they had made. They lied, saying that the money they were giving to God was the total amount of a property settlement. Peter looked at Ananias and said, "Why has Satan filled your heart to lie to the Holy Spirit . . .?" Peter must have thought, "Ananias, we had a good thing going here—maybe even the beginning of the Kingdom." All God has ever wanted is an adequate witness of His Kingdom in the earth. The early Church could have been that witness, but they began to falter. The Hebrews started murmuring against the Hellenists because their widows were being neglected in the daily distribution of provisions. Their minds were on "things" instead of spiritual unity before God.

God's heart must have been crushed. "Is this My People?" He asked. Deacons were assigned to handle the arguments between widows. Since the early Church, pastors have spent most of their time assigning committees to handle problems! The time has come to stop assigning "problem" committees, and start assigning committees with answers to share with the world.

Our consensus of opinion is of no importance to God

79

at all. God is not looking for "troubleshooters." The Church has spent its energy troubleshooting for two thousand years. God is searching for people who will put their sights on the devil and start shooting down the powers of this world so Jesus Christ can come again!

They started comparing themselves among themselves. Somebody said, "Did you know that Cephas baptized me?" "You mean Cephas baptized you!" "Well, Apollos baptized me." "I am of Paul!" "I am of Apollos!" God looked at His Church and He felt loneliness and grief. The Church had lost her power.

Why did early Christians lose their power? They lost their unity! They lost their purpose of existence! They became exclusive! "We're a white church." "We're a church that believes in circumcision." Exclusivism has no place in God's Church. Jesus waits, saying, "God, I want to find My bride." And the bride sits around arguing, debating and fussing.

Pentecost is a maturing experience, preparing us to leave our "kingdom of self" and join our spirits to the Kingdom of Christ. "Well, I spoke with tongues!" someone might say. Paul said, "Though I speak with the tongues of men and of angels, but have not love, I have become as sounding brass or a clanging cymbal" (I Corinthians 13:1). What the world has usually seen in the Charismatic movement is sounding brass and clanging cymbals. The world is still looking for something that can really make a difference.

Faith was not always strong in the early Church.

When Peter was put into prison, the Church met to pray for his release. God answered their prayer by commissioning an angel to open the prison doors and set Peter free. Peter went to the house where the prayer meeting was still in progress and knocked on the door. A girl named Rhoda answered. When she heard Peter's voice, she left him standing there and ran back inside because she got so excited. The prayer warriors said, "You are beside yourself!" Rhoda wouldn't give up so they said, "It is only Peter's angel."

People are often surprised when prayers are answered. "Faith worketh by love." The problem is, we don't have the love to implement faith. Faith becomes merely a mental game we play. Even faith requires unity which is a product of love. We have fragmented the gospel, leaving our message with no continuity. Faith cannot be exercised without love.

As our family ministered around Joan's bed a few days before she died, the Spirit of the Lord began to nudge people to whisper in Joan's ear. Her eyes would come alive as she heard our words of love. I was so conscious of the response taking place within her. She always responded to somebody saying, "I love you." Her lips would answer, "I love you." As we worshipped around her bed, Joan looked up at me. With her little, feeble hands, she started wiping away my tears. A surge of strength suddenly came into her body. She reached up and grabbed me in her arms and held me tightly.

Paul said, "I am persuaded that neither death nor life, nor angels nor principalities nor powers, nor things present nor things to come, nor height nor depth, nor any other created thing, shall be able to separate us from the love of God which is in Christ Jesus our Lord" (Romans 8:38-39). God is looking for a loving Church.

Pentecost is a prototype of the last day Church. We still lack unity, but today God is saying, "I want to bring you back to unity of faith." The Bride of Christ will love as Christ loves. She will think as Christ thinks and reach out to minister with His sensitivity.

We're told that we are surrounded by a cloud of witnesses (Hebrews 12:1). Why does the Word tell us about "the cloud"? I've been with hundreds of people when they died. Almost every dying saint I've ever prayed with has talked about seeing somebody they had known who had died previously. They have talked about seeing tremendous light.

Why did Jesus go to the mount of transfiguration? Whom did He see there? He talked with Moses and Elijah who had been dead many years. I believe that God desires interaction between planet earth and the heavenlies unlike we've ever known.

I believe that Joan is before the throne of God as one of those witnesses that the book of Hebrews talks about. She stands before God as an overcomer and intercessor urging us on. She encourages Christians on earth to be overcomers also.

The world sees the fragmentation of Christ's Body, but the Church of Jesus Christ is one. We may wear different labels, conduct our services differently, look differently on the outside, but the world and the devil will soon know that the Body of Christ is one. We are a force for God on planet earth.

We're not going to lose. We are winners for God. We must accomplish five things before Jesus Christ returns:

First of all, we discover the purpose of Pentecost. Why do we need this power? What were God's intentions in giving power to us? We cannot fragment God's plan. His plan is a constant, continuous flow of restoration. From the beginning of time until now, God has ordained a constant flow of revelation. God wants a people who will stand as a witness to the world saying, "God's character will prevail!" God's character of love will prevail over the character of satanic forces—lust, evil and greed.

Secondly, we enlarge our vision to a spiritual dimension. Individual efforts alone will never work. We enlarge our vision to spiritual proportions which include the angels. The Bible says, ". . . the angels rejoice when one is converted." "We wrestle not against flesh and blood but against powers and principalities." There's "a host" warring against us, but there's "a cloud" of witnesses cheering us on. We must broaden our perspective by saying, "God, we stand before You, the holy angels, and the powers and principalities."

Everything we do is a witness for or against the Kingdom of God. "If the spirit of Him that raised Christ from the dead dwells in you . . ." (Romans 8:11). We must accept a greater dimension of God's Spirit within us. We want the experience without the transfer of Spirit. Many people seek "an experience," but are unwilling to pay the selfless price to get the essence of Christ's character working in them.

Thirdly, we release our vision by using the keys God has given to us. Upon the revelation, "Jesus is the Christ, the Son of the living God," Jesus will build His Church. The gates of hell will not prevail against it. Jesus said He would give us the keys to the Kingdom. With that authority, whatever we bind on earth will be bound in heaven, and whatever we loose on earth will be loosed in heaven (Matthew 16:19).

Now we understand releasing His Spirit. In order for heavenly powers to be released, we must learn to take authority on planet earth. If we want to release God's love in heavenly places, release love in relationships. If we want to exercise faith on a tremendous, spiritual dimension, we must exercise faith in daily circumstances. We have the keys in our hands. Learn how to use them. That's Pentecost! When the power of the Holy Spirit is unleashed in our lives, then we have the keys of authority. We speak by faith. We move by faith. We move by God's power at a new, greater dimension.

Fourthly, we recognize that we no longer belong to ourselves. Our own wills can no longer dominate our lives. We don't lose our personalities, but now we're controlled by His Spirit. Jesus was sometimes angry at world systems and religious fallacy. He was angry at the misuse of the temple. He was moved with compassion to reach down and pick a woman accused of adultery up out of the dirt.

Pentecost is the character of God expressed through us to the world. Pentecost begins at Jerusalem, extends to Judea—those in the religious community who are similar to us; then to Samaria—those who may not understand the Spirit of God across cultural, denominational lines; and finally, to the uttermost parts of the earth.

Finally, we realize that speaking in tongues is minimal in terms of the total significance of receiving the baptism in the Holy Spirit. The tongue is a vital part of our body, but what would the tongue do alone? Pentecost affects our eyes, feet, hands—our entire bodies. Do we want the power of Pentecost? Are we willing to forfeit the right to ourselves by saying, "Spirit of Christ, rule and reign in me"? That's Pentecost! We have no right to desire the Holy Spirit if we don't understand His intentions.

When we reach the place of saying, "Holy Spirit, take over this temple," then the tongue responds properly to instructions from the heavenlies. The tongue says "yes" to God. Our words circumvent the natural mind, because the natural mind doesn't comprehend spiritual things. By the Spirit, we begin to proclaim truth in our inner man. Our words may not be beautiful, long, flowing sonnets, but the Spirit flows from us so that we say, "I want to praise You beyond my natural abilities." We are then committed to the purposes and intentions of God and to the Body of Christ. We say, "Yes, Lord, I want to receive! I want to give!"

Part 2

God's Strategy

5

JOEL'S PROPHECY

The spiritual condition of the world when Jesus was upon the earth was not the same as today. We sometimes forget that differentiation. What was the condition of the world when Jesus was here? Jesus was certainly the Messiah, but he was also a prophet who spoke to His generation. When Jesus Christ lived in Judea, He recognized that His nation was scattered all over the world. He knew that spiritually the people had turned away from God in rebellion, causing Assyria, the Chaldeans and other forces to finally take Israel and scatter her people.

No prophetic voice other than John the Baptist had spoken God's Word for many, many years. After Malachi, we must go to historical records which are not recorded in the Word of God (the Maccabeans, for instance) to know anything about Israel. Only secular historians record what took place in that interim period. No prophetic voice had spoken to Israel for all those years. Finally, John the Baptist came in the spirit of Elijah as a clear, prophetic voice.

Religion had been so desecrated that worship was based upon the traditions and commandments of men. The laws of Moses were prostituted to such an extent that Paul said, "No man could be justified by the law" (Acts 13:39). Hundreds and hundreds of laws oppressed the people: laws concerning the Sabbath, relationships, eating, and everything else imaginable.

The Jewish world was enslaved by the traditions of men. If devout Jews wanted to take a Sabbath day's journey, they sometimes obeyed the law by taking a piece of furniture, going to the end of the number of yards that they could walk on the Sabbath, and then leaving chairs. They would walk another Sabbath day's journey and leave something else. People scattered their furniture for miles on the Sabbath day to be able to say, "I didn't leave my dwelling place!" At the end of the day, they would gather all their furniture together and walk back home. That was "religion" in the day in which Jesus lived.

Jesus was a prophet. He was God's voice speaking to a world where the Jews were scattered without a prophetic voice, steeped in traditions, impossible laws and darkness. Darkness and bondage always abound without revelation. The people had no enlightenment of the Spirit. We can understand why Jesus said, "I am the light of the world." He was saying, "I have a new message for you. I have new insights for you."

Jesus observed religion in His day and said, "Worship is without form. It's void. No prophetic voice is speaking. The people honor nothing but tradition. They represent only whited sepulchres. They are merely religious people who stand on the corner in their long white robes, praying useless prayers. They are without enlightenment."

On the day of Pentecost, the Spirit of God moved to fill a spiritual void. The Jerusalem happening was the Spirit of God moving to quicken the Church and to bring life and enlightenment. Sometimes the baptism of the Holy Spirit is a misunderstood experience. Someone may be instructed, "Say this little phrase," and the response is, "I've got it!" They don't know what they have or why they have it, but "they've got it!"

The great Charismatic movement accomplished many things, but unfortunately, it also left many people frustrated because they did not receive God's power. They "claimed" the right things but had no experience of power. They didn't fully understand the purpose of Pentecost (Acts 2:15-16).

After the Holy Spirit fell upon the hundred and twenty believers on the day of Pentecost, they went from the upper room down into the streets magnifying God. Some people said that they were drunk, but Peter stood up and said, "For these are not drunk, as you suppose, since it is only the third hour of the day. But this is what was spoken by the prophet Joel." How many people at Pentecost understood Joel's prophecy? All Peter did was quote the Book of Joel. Peter said, "This was 'that' . . ." If we are going to understand the Jerusalem happening, we must understand Joel's revelation.

The word of the Lord for the elders came to Joel saying, "The land is wasted." Joel also saw the earth without form and structure as it was at creation. God's authority did not exist. The earth was dying and desolate. Joel knew that the land was in need of help. He cried out, "Awake!"

Has the world ever been as desolate as it is today? Has it ever been more confused than it is now? Do we realize that enough power has already been harnessed to destroy every living thing on planet earth? Only one group of people—God's people—can bring about a solution. Scientists and intellectuals can't do it. The land is wasted. Many people sit around waiting for God to do something when God has made his purposes very clear, "I'm going to give you power. I'm going to give you authority at Pentecost so you can fulfill Joel's prophecy."

Awake, you drunkards, and weep; and wail, all you drinkers of wine, because of the new wine, for it has been cut off from your mouth. For a nation has come up against My land. (Joel 1:5-6)

Lament like a virgin girded with sackcloth for the husband of her youth. The grain offering and the drink offering have been cut off from the house of the Lord; the priests mourn, who minister to the Lord. (Joel 1:8-9)

Be ashamed, you farmers, wail, you vinedressers, for the wheat and the barley; because the harvest of the field has perished. The vine has dried up, and the fig tree has withered; the pomegranate tree, the palm tree also, and the apple tree—all the trees of the field are withered; surely joy has withered away from the sons of men. (Joel 1:11-12)

People travel to the oceans, the mountains and all over the world just to find fleeting moments of joy. Comedians entertain all over the world just to help people find a little laughter which lasts only moments. Do we realize how much money and energy people spend simply pursuing a little pleasure?

Joel addressed the problems of his day when he said that the joy had departed. "Gird yourselves and lament, you priests . . . Come, lie all night in sackcloth . . . Consecrate a fast, call a sacred assembly . . . And cry out to the Lord" (Joel 1:13-14).

My spirit becomes so burdened with this passage. Oh, that the Holy Spirit would pull back the veil! We sit around stargazing, wondering if God is going to do something. Meanwhile, God said, "I've given you everything you need. I've given you authority to bind and to loose." He that is within us is greater than he that is in the world. We sit around saying, "Come, Lord Jesus, and do it for us," and Jesus is held as a hostage in the heavens because we are not doing our jobs (Acts 3:21).

God spoke to Solomon saying,

When I shut up heaven and there is no rain, or command the locusts to devour the land, or send pestilence among My people, if My people who are called by My name will humble themselves, and pray and seek My face, and turn from their wicked ways, then I will hear from heaven, and will forgive their sin and heal their land. (II Chronicles 7:13-14)

"I will forgive your trespasses. I will heal your land." This healing includes Ethiopia as well as any other desolate place on the earth. By prophetic voices and God's authority, He can do mighty things if we will only understand that His power is ready to be released. But we have made excuses and have put the responsibility on someone else's shoulders.

Joel delivered a prophecy of doom and defeat. "The food is cut off. There is no joy or gladness. The storehouses are in shambles." What are the storehouses? Malachi said, "Bring all the tithes into the storehouse" (Malachi 3:10). The storehouse is God's habitation. God is doing His Kingdom work from the storehouses. If the Church does her job, mammon will serve us. If we do our job of excellency as we should in television, drama and the arts, the world will lay their treasures at our feet.

Joseph is a symbol of the Church. Why was Joseph second in command in Egypt? He had a creative mentality; he knew how to give answers when they should be given. He was able to say, "I know how to solve the drought problems. I know what to do when famine comes." Daniel also became notable in the Kingdom. By the Spirit, he understood the handwriting on the wall. He was a man who knew the day in which he lived.

Instead we spend our money for that which produces no food. We go to the entertainment houses of the world when the world should be knocking at our doors. This mentality is what Pentecost is all about. Unless we understand the condition of the world that Joel addressed, the Holy Spirit's coming has little or no meaning at all.

O Lord, to You I cry out; for fire has devoured the open pastures, and a flame has burned all the trees of the field. The beasts of the field also cry out to You, for the water brooks are dried up, and fire has devoured the open pastures. (Joel 1:19-20)

All creation is groaning, waiting for deliverance from the bondage of corruption. Joel's prophecy is the key to the purpose of the Holy Spirit's coming. The earth is groaning for the manifestation of the power of God in His Church. For too long the Church has sat around like "a knot on a log," not knowing what is going on. Meanwhile, God is saying, "Listen! Listen! Wake up! Wake up! This is your hour, Church!" The whole earth is groaning, waiting for the manifestation of God's Spirit through human vessels.

The Church must sound the trumpet. The world will not do it. The world will mock us. Regardless of that, the Church must wake up. On many occasions I have lain awake all night long. I have battled for days saying, "God, in my flesh I want so much to end our national television ministry. I get weary with the constant pressures and demands. I don't want to be troubled with it anymore." But God would answer me,

"Who will sound the trumpet in Zion?"

Blow the trumpet in Zion, and sound an alarm in My holy mountain! Let all the inhabitants of the land tremble; for the day of the Lord is coming, for it is at hand: a day of darkness and gloominess, a day of clouds and thick darkness . . . A fire devours before them, and behind them a flame burns. (Joel 2:1-3)

If that description doesn't depict the atomic age, then I don't know what does. Before the atomic bomb was dropped, the Japanese landscape was described as beautiful pastureland with lovely foliage. Afterwards, however, the land was drastically changed into a charred wilderness that fire had destroyed. Joel 2:6 says, "The people writhed in pain. All faces are drained of color." Have you ever looked at the faces of victims of Viet Nam or people in the drug culture? Have you looked at the countryside where bombs have fallen?

If young people would only look at the faces of those who are on drugs, they would know how horrible drug abuse is. Drug abusers are without facial expression and joy. They walk around bleary-eyed. At a hospital some time ago, a beautiful eighteen-year-old girl who had used drugs came up to me and asked, "Are you my daddy?" An attendant gently took her by the hand and led her back to her room.

"The Lord gives voice before His army, for His camp is very great; for strong is the One who executes His word. For the day of the Lord is great and very terrible; who can endure it?" (Joel 2:11). In the last days God will assemble a mighty army, knitted together one bone to another. The same Spirit of God that moved at Pentecost will breathe on the army and it will come alive. This is the day that God talked about. He is beginning to breathe Pentecostal fire. Why? So we can find "that which was lost" and recover it, so we can judge the world of sin, so Jesus can come back to claim His own.

Pentecost can never happen within us until we repent. We must say, "God, forgive me for my careless-ness and callousness. Forgive me for my self-centered life. Forgive me for not understanding who the Church is. Forgive me for not knowing why You gave children to me." The way most children turn out today, we shouldn't rejoice when a womb is alive. We should re-joice when a womb is barren, when the quiver is empty. Many Christian families lose their children to the world when they are ten or twelve years old.

> *Who knows if He will turn and relent, and leave a blessing behind Him—a grain offering and a drink offering for the Lord your God? Blow the trumpet in Zion, consecrate a fast, call a sacred assembly; gather the people, sanctify the congregation, assemble the elders, gather the children and nursing babes; let the bridegroom go out from his chamber, and the bride from her dressing room. Let the priests, who minister to the Lord, weep between the porch and the altar; let them say, "Spare Your people, O Lord, and do not give Your heritage to reproach, that the nations should rule over them. Why should they say among the peoples, 'Where is their God?'" (Joel 2:14-17)*

This scripture does not refer to natural Israel. The book of Revelation describes this same army of people. When John lists the twelve tribes, He does not list them according to the Judaistic tradition of naming the eldest son first. Had he done so, Reuben would have been named first, but the list begins instead with Judah, whose descendants are of the household of David. This lineage represents the tabernacle of praise and the habitation of God. People are looking toward the Middle East when they need to see God's people all over the earth.

> *Then the Lord will be zealous for His land, and pity His people. The Lord will answer and say to His people, "Behold, I will send you grain and new wine and oil, and you will be satisfied by them; I will no longer make you a reproach among the nations." (Joel 2:18-19)*

Joel was prophesying about the gift of the Holy Ghost. He was talking about having lamps which are trimmed with oil. The Spirit of God is moving. We have seen the early rain, but the latter rain is now beginning to fall. My mother received the baptism of the Holy Spirit when she was only twelve years old, and she was one of the first Spirit-filled Methodists in the state of Georgia. I know where we came from and how we have moved through the Charismatic period. We are now entering the time when the Kingdom message must be preached. This is the hour when we must know the reason the Holy Spirit has been poured out upon us.

> *Fear not, O land; be glad and rejoice, for the Lord has done marvelous things! . . . For He has given you the former rain faithfully, and He will cause the rain to come down for you—the former rain, and the latter rain in the first month. So I will restore to you the years that the swarming locust has eaten . . . (Joel 2:21,23,25)*

Joel talked about restoration, the outpouring of the Spirit and David's tabernacle of praise. Unless we demonstrate the essence of real worship, we will miss a great opportunity. Worship is not how high one jumps or how loud one yells. Worship is an internal experience with God. Denominational lines are disappearing and God is restoring His people as the oil of praise is being poured out.

The following part of Joel's prophecy was quoted by Peter:

And it shall come to pass afterward that I will pour out My Spirit on all flesh; your sons and your daughters shall prophesy, your old men shall dream dreams, your young men shall see visions; and also on My menservants and on My maidservants I will pour out My Spirit in those days. And I will show wonders in the heavens and in the earth: blood and fire and pillars of smoke. The sun shall be turned into darkness, and the moon into blood, before the coming of the great and terrible day of the Lord. (Joel 2:28-31)

The worldly enlightenment of this day will end. Joel prophesied that even the intellectuals of this day will be confounded. God's servants will experience greater spiritual enlightenment. Worldly systems will collapse, but God will show signs in the heavens. His people will begin to take control of the elements. Ethiopia is experiencing famine only because they do not have a prophet. If the Church understood her mission, she would raise up prophets to stand in the face of the enemy. Even in godless, Communistic nations, prophets would be able to say, "Thus saith the Lord. It is not going to rain until you get on your face and repent."

Until the Elijah spirit returns to the Church, Jesus Christ cannot come again. Before Jesus Christ could come in the flesh, John the Baptist prepared the way by prophesying in the spirit of Elijah. John's ministry was a prototype of what the Church must become for the Lord to return. When we move with Pentecostal power and God's authority by taking dominion and sitting with Him in heavenly places, we will begin to rule and reign with Him. Then He can say, "It is time for the marriage supper of the Lamb." Jesus Christ will never come until the Bride is mature.

We often hear from people who are meeting together to watch our programs on television. They say, "We are under great persecution, but your ministry teaches spiritual truth. We are still going to our churches. Sometimes we feel 'beaten over the head,' but we have an army of people here who understand what you are preaching. When you blow the trumpet, we come forth! We are going to obey God's voice."

And it shall come to pass that whoever calls on the name of the Lord shall be saved. For in Mount Zion and in Jerusalem there shall be deliverance, as the Lord has said, among the remnant whom the Lord calls. (Joel 2:32)

God will judge the nations of the earth. The Church must become a standard so God can judge the world. God searches for a standard. He is a God who is just. He must show the world a Kingdom demonstration.

Wasn't that God's intention with Job? God said, "Have you noticed My servant Job? He is a righteous man. He is a standard for his generation." Job is a type of the Church. The devil said, "Let me get to him. I will show you that he will not last." God backed off and the devil inflicted sickness on Job. A price is always paid for commitment, and commitment will be tested. As surely as a seed is sown in the soil, tribulation will come. Many people give up whenever tribulation begins.

We are approaching the period of time in which the Church will judge the world by becoming God's standard. How can we be a standard of order when there is no structure in the Church? How can we be a standard of oneness when divisions exist in the Body of Christ? Will Jesus Christ come back for a divided Body? The Baptists are on one side of the street, the Methodists on the other side, and Pentecostals are down the road. Everybody accuses everybody else. Meanwhile, Jesus is interceding, "O Father, let them be one that the world may know Me." How many people God requires for a standard, I do not know, but He will raise up enough people that He can judge the world.

A measurement can only be accurate if there is "a yardstick" to judge it. God cannot judge the world until He has a witness, a Kingdom demonstration. "And this gospel of the kingdom will be preached in all the world as a witness to all the nations, and then the end will come" (Matthew 24:14). The demonstration—the standard—is not yet recognized by the world. According to Joel, the next move after the outpouring of the Holy Spirit is the judgment of the nations of the earth.

I will also gather all nations, and bring them down to the Valley of Jehoshaphat; and I will enter into judgment with them there on account of My people, My heritage Israel, whom they have scattered among the nations; they have also divided up My land. They have cast lots for My people, have given a boy in exchange for a harlot, and sold a girl for wine, that they may drink. (Joel 3:2-3)

Warfare is inevitable where truth is preached. Teaching on minor issues will be blown out of proportion and debated. The devil will come against God's people, especially those proclaiming truth. Satan will try to drive God's people into bankruptcy. He will manipulate them into improper relationships. He will try to distort their thinking. Satan doesn't care if we get involved in time-consuming, religious activities. A church can have a great softball team or a choir with beautiful robes. A church can do things that people think are great and wonderful, but those things generally do not threaten Satan's kingdom. When Satan sees the Church demonstrating the principles of the Kingdom, he becomes riled and feels threatened.

Because you have taken My silver and My gold, and have carried into your temples My prized possessions. (Joel 3:5)

God's people have carried His silver, gold and prized possessions and placed them in strange temples. People take money which God intended to establish His Kingdom and patronize other kingdoms. People spend money on things that have no value—no ultimate good. Money is spent on frivolities while the Kingdom of God suffers, unable to pay its bills. The hour has come to say, "The Kingdom of God is at hand." The hour has come to ask, "Lord, what can I do? Where can I invest my energy?" If someone were told that he had only one month to live, what would he do with it? "Have you taken My gold and silver and put it in other temples? Have you spent the tithe on things that have no value?"

Joel preached, "Let the weak say, 'I am strong' " (Joel 3:10). That teaching is the foundation of speaking "the word" of faith. Faith ignites the power and authority God puts within us. God said, "Let the nations be awakened, and come up to the Valley of Jehoshaphat; for there I will sit to judge all the surrounding nations" (Joel 3:12). This scripture is not describing some valley in the Middle East. This passage refers to the Church who is becoming God's witness to the nations.

The hour of decision is upon us. What will we do with our time and talents? What will we do with our energies? The world is waiting. This world can't survive if the Church does not move boldly forward. God is looking for a "Joseph" Church so that His blessings can flow to all people.

And it will come to pass in that day that the mountains shall drip with new wine, the hills shall flow with milk, and all the brooks of Judah shall be flooded with water; a fountain shall flow from the house of the Lord and water the Valley of Acacias. (Joel 3:18)

Praise [Judah] will bring a fountain of life to the house of God. Egypt, which represents the law, the legalities of life, will be desolate (Joel 3:19). The law kills, but the Spirit makes alive.

Repeatedly I am asked, "What is the success of Chapel Hill Harvester Church?" I tell people that Chapel Hill's ministry is not built on preaching or singing. Our witness is based on the ability of God's people to emerge from legalistic attitudes. God blesses churches where people surrender their lives to Him so that He can use them as temples of the Holy Spirit.

I understand the reasons some men of God in scripture hid in caves or sat under juniper trees. They often became weary and frustrated. Tremendous pressures rest on pastors today. I wonder how many people discern the times in which they live? How many people know that this is the day of the Lord? Several years ago, a band came out of England and captivated the whole world. Another young singer comes along who whines and whispers and wears strange clothes, and the whole world seeks him. He soon possesses the hearts of young people. Who are we following?

Peter stood up on the day of Pentecost and boldly preached, "This is what was spoken by the prophet Joel." The Holy Spirit brings healing, recovery and rejoicing. This experience of power puts an end to Satan's domain in one's life. The Jerusalem happening is that experience giving the Church the authority and power to cast out devils and heal the sick. Deliverance will come through the Church, the New Jerusalem, unless a person's death would yield a greater benefit for the Kingdom than their living. Prayers of faith will heal the sick. I have said to God, "If dying before the time pleasing to my flesh could enhance the Kingdom of God, then let me go home."

Why are we living? Why are we existing? Do we live to obtain a great education and make a lot of money? Do we live to buy a big house? Do we live to amass riches so others can eventually fight over them? Living for the Kingdom of God is what living is all about. True living is finding "that which is lost," setting young people on the right path, looking into confused eyes and having the ability to speak truth to them. True living is giving the world a standard of love.

We must understand that we are not just some "little housewife," or some "little service station attendant." We are offsprings of God. We are establishing God's purposes on this planet. We are called of God for such an hour as this. I want to see God's Word sweep across the country. My major concern is seeing Jesus. I want to see this world corrected and God on His throne on earth as He is in heaven. I want to see Babylon fall. I want to see the great mammon system fail. I long to see the glory of God cover the earth. "The earth is the Lord's, and all its fullness" (Psalm 24:1). "Let everything that has breath praise the Lord" (Psalm 150:6).

6

THE STANDARD

Who are God's vinedressers on the earth today? God placed Adam and Eve in the garden and told them to dress and take care of their domain. Our charge is no different in the world today. God has never changed His plan. What are we doing to improve the environment where God has placed us? Jesus told the Jews, the chief priests and Pharisees, that they had rejected a task given to them from the Son of God Himself. "He came to His own, and His own did not receive Him" (John 1:11).

Jesus said to them, "Did you never read in the Scriptures: 'The stone which the builders rejected has become the chief cornerstone. This was the Lord's doing, and it is

marvelous in our eyes'? Therefore I say to you, the king-
dom of God will be taken from you and given to a nation
bearing the fruits of it." But when they sought to lay
hands on Him, they feared the multitudes, because they
took Him for a prophet. (Matthew 21:42-43;46)

A continuing ministry in both Old and New Testament times is the ministry of the prophet. A prophet is
either accepted or he is stoned. He is either loved and
honored or hated and killed. One must either accept the
ministry of a prophet or totally reject it. A prophetic
word leaves no middle ground because it requires a
decision calling for people to pay a price in their lives.

Some people argue that no prophets minister today
except through the spirit of prophecy, but God assigned
prophets to the Church (I Corinthians 12:28). The spirit
of prophecy, the gift of prophecy and the office of a
prophet are distinctly different according to God's
Word.

God has called apostles, prophets, evangelists, pastors and teachers in the Church. If pastors minister
today, so do apostles and prophets. Prophets have usually been rejected by their own generations. Jesus
Christ was no exception.

Jesus Christ is the standard by which every nation
will be judged. Nations will not be judged by whether
they knew God Jehovah and obeyed the Ten Commandments. They will be judged by whether Jesus
Christ was their stumbling block or their cornerstone.
That standard of judgment has been true for two thousand years. Jesus said that He came first to the house

of Israel, but they rejected Him. Therefore, Jesus turned to anyone who would accept Him by faith.

"Hear another parable: There was a certain landowner who planted a vineyard and set a hedge around it, dug a winepress in it and built a tower. And he leased it to vinedressers and went into a far country. Now when vintage-time drew near, he sent his servants to the vinedressers, that they might receive its fruit. And the vinedressers took his servants, beat one, killed one, and stoned another. Again he sent other servants, more than the first, and they did likewise to them. Then last of all he sent his son [Jesus Christ] to them, saying, 'They will respect my son.' But when the vinedressers saw the son, they said among themselves, 'This is the heir. Come, let us kill him and seize his inheritance.' And they caught him, and cast him out of the vineyard, and killed him. Therefore, when the owner of the vineyard comes, what will he do to those vinedressers? They said to Him, 'He will destroy those wicked men miserably, and lease his vineyard to other vinedressers who will render to him the fruits in their seasons.' " (Matthew 21:33-41)

One point of this parable is that God always sends ambassadors to proclaim His truth. He invariably reaches out to find people who understand what He wants them to do on the earth. He put Adam and Eve here as His offspring to replenish the earth. Jesus came to fulfill a specific mission of restoration. The human spirit can only be brought alive again in Jesus Christ.

We must be children of faith. Through Jesus Christ, we return obedience to planet earth. Our obedience to God recovers that which was lost. Whatever was lost through rebellion is restored through the seed of Jesus

Christ in His Church. Our obedience restores the earth to the place God intended it to be in the beginning.

God has subjected Himself to His own plan of recovery. In God's omnipotent and omniscient sovereignty, He has subjected Himself to His own words. God said, "I will make man in My own image." He said in Revelation, "I stand at the door and knock." God in His sovereign plan says, "I will not intrude into your life. I will entreat you. I will invite you, but I will not force My will on you." Sinners can even go unchecked. Sowing to their flesh, they eventually reap corruption. God will not intrude into our minds. We must open our hearts to Him. God has imposed His own plan upon Himself.

Jesus demonstrated total obedience in the flesh. Everything He did was within the will of His Father. Prayer guided His activities and His words. He was ready to obey, totally in step with the Father. We can never fulfill God's plan on planet earth without total obedience to God.

Jesus Christ is our standard. He is the firstfruit of the Church. Now corporately we must learn obedience as Jesus Christ did. If the Church is called to continue the mission that Jesus began, then the Church must continue to seek and to save that which was lost. The Church must continue to heal and to restore. Jesus has sent the Holy Spirit to complete His mission through us. Paradise was lost and people were lost because of the sin of the world. We, the Church, are in the process of dealing with that sin.

Continuing incarnation means that we are the Body

of Christ upon the earth. The concept of "God in the flesh" sometimes frightens people. The most exciting realization in my life is that I am "a Jesus." I don't need to literally die on the cross for my sins. Jesus has already done that for mankind. But I can live out the principles of self-denial by "taking up my cross" and saying with Paul, "I die daily." I can become God's vessel of obedience on the earth.

In the early days of Pentecost in this century, Christians thought that the ultimate spiritual experience was exuberance and joy. People came to church from working long hours in the cotton fields and textile mills. They were weary and tired until they began to sing and praise God. The Holy Spirit would fall and God's glory would refresh them. The Holy Spirit supplied whatever they needed to receive from God.

God has brought us today to a deeper understanding of our mission as His people. The Holy Spirit is given to the Church to empower us to live out the restoration which Jesus Christ began. The Holy Spirit empowers the Church to continue what Christ began to do and to teach, proclaiming the Kingdom of God.

Now it came to pass in those days that He went out to the mountain to pray, and continued all night in prayer to God. And when it was day, He called His disciples to Him; and from them He chose twelve whom He also named apostles. (Luke 6:12-13)

Before Jesus ascended to the Father, He chose people to carry on His work. They were told to "tarry in Jerusalem until . . ." The Jerusalem happening triggered the final stage of God's recovery of planet earth.

"To whom He also presented Himself alive after His suffering by many infallible proofs, being seen by them during forty days and speaking of the things pertaining to the kingdom of God" (Acts 1:3). For forty days He taught them truths pertaining to the Kingdom of God—the establishment of His reign on earth.

And being assembled together with them, He commanded them not to depart from Jerusalem, but to wait for the Promise of the Father, "which," He said, "you have heard from Me; for John truly baptized with water, but you shall be baptized with the Holy Spirit not many days from now." Therefore when they had come together, they asked Him, saying, "Lord, will You at this time restore the kingdom to Israel?" (Acts 1:4-6)

Why did they ask Him, "Will You at this time restore the Kingdom?" They had heard Him teach for forty days about His Kingdom. How is the Kingdom going to come? How are we going to restore the earth? So naturally they asked Him, "Are you going to do that now, Jesus?"

Take note of the question, "Are you at this time going to restore the kingdom to Israel?" Notice, they were thinking about God's promises to King David. They were thinking about the twelve tribes, national Israel. But what did Jesus say to them?

And He said to them, "It is not for you to know times or seasons which the Father has put in His own authority. But you shall receive power when the Holy Spirit has come upon you; and you shall be witnesses to Me in Jerusalem, and in all Judea and Samaria, and to the end of the earth." (Acts 1:7-8)

The total view of God's plan includes much more than national Israel. The witness begins in Jerusalem, but it goes to Judea and Samaria and to the uttermost parts of the earth. Jesus' message is world encompassing. Jesus told them to forget about the times, seasons, and their tunnel vision for their own nation.

A great problem in the Church today is the lack of discernment. Too many pastors lack the boldness to say, "That spirit is not of God!" The mark of the mature Church is the ability to discern between religious spirits and the leading of the Holy Spirit. Until the Church exercises discernment, it cannot change the world. Many ministries—under the guise of Christianity—are nothing more than frustrated religious spirits. Jesus said, "I will give My Church the power to loose and to bind. I will give you authority and discernment."

Quietness in a church service gives opportunity for the Holy Spirit to express Himself. Almost inevitably in those moments, religious spirits will manifest themselves also. The Church needs authority, particularly in large congregations, who knows the difference between manifestations of religious spirits, false prophetic spirits and prophetic utterances which are of God. If we don't have that authority in eldership, the Church doesn't have a chance. Someone with a religious spirit always wants to exalt himself to seek attention.

Why did Jesus want His Church to release power?

What was "power from on high" intended to do? He gave us power to recover lost territory, to "seek and to save that which was lost." We should recover whatever was lost to the devil. We lost our dominion over planet earth. We lost the kingdom of art and the kingdom of music. We lost . . . we lost . . . we lost . . . God says that by the power of the Holy Spirit we can regain lost territory. Every good and perfect gift comes from Him. The devil has prostituted creation and the Church has rejected things of beauty that really belong to God. We must reclaim everything that was lost to restore the earth to His Kingdom.

The Holy Spirit gives the Church power to deal with rebellion and disobedience. That responsibility belongs to spiritual authority in the Church. When the concept of spiritual authority is taught, many people become uncomfortable. Just because spiritual authority is desecrated by "Jim Jones" types, we must not disregard the truth of authority in the Church.

We need authority to judge the world of sin—to establish standards of righteousness. Someone brought a demon-possessed, blind and mute man to Jesus. With great authority, Jesus delivered the man of the demon, restoring both sight and speech to the man. The multitudes were amazed at God's power, but the Pharisees were enraged.

But Jesus knew their thoughts, and said to them: "Every kingdom divided against itself is brought to desolation, and every city or house divided against itself will not stand. And if Satan casts out Satan, he is divided against himself. How then will his kingdom stand? And if I cast out demons by Beelzebub, by whom do your sons cast them out? Therefore they shall be your judges. But if I cast out demons by the Spirit of God, surely the kingdom of God has come upon you." (Matthew 12:25-28)

The purpose of the Holy Spirit is to empower us with authority over demonic forces, to recover from the devil what has been snatched away for his destructive purposes. The Bible says that Satan comes to steal, to kill and to destroy. If we are to be children of God, the seed of the resurrection, the sons of obedience, we must learn to prevent Satan from killing, stealing and destroying.

Parents should be aware of where their children are and what they are doing. Satan wants to steal our young people. Why do we have the Holy Spirit? Just to talk in tongues? Oh, no! We need God's power to claim our boys and girls for the Kingdom of God.

God's strategy is to use the witness principle to establish His standard on planet earth. God is a just God. How does He judge? I say to young people, "Don't let the world set standards for you." If a fad of the world is to roll rather than to walk, many people will get down on the ground to roll. Our children are breaking their backs "break dancing." The point is, why do people do what they are doing?

The time has come for God's people to follow the Holy Spirit by developing godly attitudes and exemplary standards. The Church is God's standard to the world. The world says "sell" and God says "give." The world is waiting to see a body of people who truly walk in

115

faith and disregard worldly systems. The Church is to become the standard by which the world is judged. How dare we let the world judge and influence the Church?

False angels surround God's people. We are about to enter into warfare like we have never known before. Revelation says prophets will come with false religions, calling down fire from heaven and bringing images to life. Without the discerning power of the Holy Spirit, God's people can easily be deceived.

What can we do about this matter of discernment? We need to develop a Kingdom mentality. We must not have the mentality that Peter spoke about— ". . . all things continue as they were" (II Peter 3:4). That attitude must be challenged. Just because no previous generation has ever overcome death does not mean a generation will not conquer "the last enemy."

"Therefore, if you died with Christ from the basic principles of the world, why, as though living in the world, do you subject yourselves to regulations . . ." (Colossians 2:20). This scripture asks us an important question. If we have died with Christ and have reckoned ourselves to be dead to the world, why are we still following man's concepts and standards? The commandments of men are, "Do not touch, do not taste, do not handle."

If we are freed through Christ, why do we continue to be intimidated by "do not touch, do not handle, do not taste"? Social standards are commandments and doctrines of men. Social standards have an appearance of wisdom, but in reality they are humanistic, self-imposed religion.

False humility and personal neglect in order to look like saints is the practice of Pharisees. False humility has nothing to do with living for Christ. We should give ourselves to God's will. We need to reject the commandments and traditions of men. We must receive God's revelation by practicing a Kingdom mentality, releasing the power of God in our lives.

Why are we living? Do our goals focus on a paycheck? Where do we set our priorities? Paying doctors' bills, dentists' bills or car repairs?

Our lives should be focused on regaining lost paradise—thinking like God wants us to think, seeing more than just the circumstances. We need to be aware of that heavenly host who surrounds us. We must be confident that we are overcoming the powers of Satan. For example, writers should concentrate on regaining any area lost to God's Kingdom in literature. Musicians should regain whatever has been lost in the kingdom of music. Technicians should regain their particular fields for God's Kingdom. Songwriters should concentrate their energies toward regaining whatever has been lost to Satan in lyrics which gratify the flesh instead of the spirit. The Church should be in the business of restoring God's paradise.

Jesus said to the rich young ruler who asked Him how to inherit eternal life, "You lack one thing. Sell all that you have and give it to the poor." Jesus required this response from the young man because Jesus discerned his attachment to material things. When our assets are usable to accomplish God's purposes, then God can trust us with wealth. As long as riches rule us and we constantly strive for greater wealth, God can never trust us with prosperity. But people who seek first the Kingdom of God can become channels through which God can accomplish His purposes. God willingly blesses those people with talent, influence and authoritative positions.

True life means overcoming sin in the world through faith. Obedience means overcoming sin by setting up a Kingdom by which God can judge the world. When a person changes the circumstances around him—casts out devils by discernment and walks in a life of obedience before the Lord—he is one who understands Pentecost. The Spirit of the Jerusalem happening must spread around the world. The power of the Holy Spirit must live within us as His temples.

Why do we need the Holy Spirit? We need His power to bring us to the image of Christ; to be able to use our God-given talents; to set the standard by which God can judge the world!

7

JUDGING THE WORLD RULER

Satan is the ruler of the principalities and the powers of the air. He does not own the earth. He is an intruder on the earth who must be cast out. The Holy Spirit is given to the Church to bring judgment to the world.

Old denominational theories claim the world will be lost through fire. If we never enjoy the earth in eternity, what is the reason to judge Satan? Those who believe that theory would be consistent in praying Satan does his destructive work quickly so that Jesus can come, but that is not the teaching of the Bible. Pentecost brings power to judge the ruler of this world.

Satanic forces are greatly evident through the god of mammon. Mammon is a world ruler. The Babylon spirit, the spirit of commerce, rules many nations and individual lives. John said that the lust of the flesh, the lust of the eyes, and the pride of life are gods of this world. Those sins are obvious. Satan enters into our imaginations and spirits through our minds. He attacks us through our thought processes, our soulish desires and our consciousness. Until we change our thought processes, attitudes and ability to believe truth, God cannot operate through us.

Merely hearing the Word will not complete God's plan of redemption. Doing the Word brings completion. Wordly disasters occur, but they do not determine end time events. Wars, famines and earthquakes are only the beginning of sorrows (Mark 13:8). The end of satanic rule and the beginning of Jesus Christ's rule and reign is when the Gospel of the Kingdom has been preached and demonstrated.

Confrontations between worldly systems and right-eous people are necessary. Confrontations will end when the Church becomes God's witness standard for God to judge Satan. The ruler of principalities and powers of the air and systems of this world will not be judged by merely hearing the Gospel of the Kingdom. When the Gospel of the Kingdom has been demon-strated as a witness, then God in His righteousness can judge the ruler of this world.

Hearing and understanding God's Word instead of circumstances or men's opinions, activate the Word which grows within us. We must hear God's Word and see His plan more clearly than man's ideas. Then we can judge worldly concepts by Jesus Christ. His life becomes the standard of our success. Jesus was "a doer" of the Word. The Holy Spirit will never force us to comply with God's Word. Only when we say, "Thy will be done," do we open ourselves to the Holy Spirit to perform His work.

Spiritual results in the world today require that our lives have genuine evidence of Jesus Christ in us. Otherwise, the Holy Spirit cannot act. Two ingredients must be evident before the Holy Spirit can complete His mission on earth.

Only anointed ears will understand by the Spirit. The natural mind cannot comprehend that the Holy Spirit is absolutely enslaved by disunity and unable to function until unity exists among members of Christ's Body. Jesus prayed that the world would see unity in His body to know that He came (John 17). Jesus assigned the five-fold ministry to the Church "for the unity of faith."

Ezekiel saw a vision of scattered bones. He obediently prophesied the word of the Lord and the Spirit of God brought the bones together into a viable body. The Holy Spirit always brings unity. The day of Pentecost was unique because God's people were in one place and in one accord. The Holy Spirit was poured out because they were unified. That experience has happened, but it must happen repeatedly. Pentecost must occur in the last days with a new joining of dry bones. Ezekiel saw a last day revelation of scattered bones. When these bones came together by the prophetic word of God, unity allowed the Holy Spirit to do His work.

Body-life ministry is when the Church joins in unity for God to do His work. The Holy Spirit cannot work any other way. What God demonstrated through Jesus Christ personally must be demonstrated in the Body of Christ corporately.

The gifts of the Spirit operate by one spirit in one body (I Corinthians 12). No part of the body can say, "I have no need of another part." The Holy Spirit in Jesus Christ worked in one body. The Holy Spirit now must work in a unified body also if the Spirit is to be released.

How can the Spirit of God work in a city like Atlanta or even in a county? How can God work on a worldwide scale when the bones are scattered? A certain church emphasizes one thing. Another church emphasizes something else. All are worthy endeavors—emphasizing Little League, basketball, or a home for unwed mothers. But the Body of Christ will be knit together only in one single thrust. The Church with a single voice means unity in the Body of Christ.

What can we do? I believe when we understand who we are as one Body and move with one spirit, the Holy Spirit will surely lead us. The Holy Spirit can lead us to triumph over circumstances. We become a victorious Church when we become a unified force on Earth. Unity is necessary for the operation of the Holy Spirit.

The gifts of the Spirit are meaningless without love. Immediately following I Corinthians 12, which lists the gifts of the Spirit, is a chapter on love. Every gift that we have is useless unless it ministers with love. How can a God of love trust a powerful gift of miracles to someone who does not have love for the Body of Christ? How can God trust a spirit of discernment to someone who does not discern with love? A discerning mind looks into the innermost being of a person. Unity and love are necessary in order for God's power and spirit to work. Scattered bones of the Church prevent a revival of God's power in the world today. God is saying, "Let prophecy go forth. Let the Spirit move! Let the bones be knit together to become a mighty army! This is the day of God's mighty army!"

Jesus said:

But now I go away to Him who sent Me, and none of you asks Me, 'Where are You going?' But because I have said these things to you, sorrow has filled your heart. Nevertheless, I tell you the truth. It is to your advantage that I go away; for if I do not go away, the Helper will not come to you; but if I depart, I will send Him to you.

And when He has come, He will convict the world of sin, of righteousness, and of judgment: of sin, because they do not believe in Me; of righteousness, because I go to My Father and you see Me no more; of judgment, because the ruler of this world is judged. (John 16:5-11)

We must realize that the Church will put Satan into the bottomless pit forever. The Church will prove that Lucifer is wrong. Lucifer has been defeated by the cross, but he is still active and powerful. I am convinced that in his own mind, Lucifer believes he is going to win. He is deceived. Although he knows that Jesus took the keys of death, hell, and the grave, Satan, who once challenged the throne of God, assumes that he can do it again. Satan works in the Church because he believes he can overcome the Church. He thinks the Church will never become a demonstration of Jesus Christ. By the authority of Jesus Christ, I declare that the Church will become a demonstration of Him and capture the devil's territory! The Church will soon be shaken. Her bones will come alive, and she will judge the ruler of this world.

One reason the Church has not reached full maturity is that preachers have not searched for understanding of the Holy Spirit's purpose. The Jerusalem experience brings judgment against the ruler of this world. Jesus said, "I am going to endue you with power; I am going to bring Kingdom authority to you." The Holy Spirit came for the correction of the earth, to judge Lucifer and the systems of this world, and to bring Christ back to earth as Lord and King. Jesus said, "I have many things to say to you, but you cannot bear them now." That is the reason God's prophets preach two thousand years later.

Many people feel no need for further revelation or fresh revelation. God's Word never even suggests an end to further insights. If someone adds to or deletes from the revelation of Jesus Christ, he will be judged. However, fresh, continuing revelation is necessary today for insights into the mysteries of the Kingdom. Why did Jesus speak mysteries in parables? Jesus said, "By the Spirit, I will unfold mysteries to you." By the Holy Spirit, God is causing a mighty rain of revelation in His Church today.

Jesus told His disciples that He had many things to tell them. "However, when He, the Spirit of truth has come, He will guide you into all truth; for He will not speak on His own authority, but whatever He hears He will speak; and He will tell you things to come" (John 16:13).

Some people believe that prophecy is not for today. They believe no new things can be learned about spiritual truth. Why has the Holy Spirit come if He is going to tell us only things that are in the Bible? The Holy Spirit brings fresh insights and fresh revelation to guide us into truth and to judge and defeat Satan. The Holy Spirit tells us future events. He glorifies Jesus, declaring His will. A mature Body of Christ will listen and act upon His words. "All things that the Father has are Mine. Therefore I said that He will take of Mine and declare it to you" (John 16:15).

The world is under the sway of Satan. The earth is like a man intoxicated with alcohol. "We know that we are of God, and the whole world lies under the sway of the wicked one" (I John 5:19). Almost every system of the world has ulterior motives because of satanic influences. At the base of all debauchery is greed and the kingdom of self. At the root of worldliness is selfishness and the appetites of our own flesh.

Because of the influences of Satan, the world listens to the antichrist spirit. "You are of God, little children, and have overcome them, because He who is in you is greater than he who is in the world. They are of the world. Therefore they speak as of the world, and the world hears them" (I John 4:4-5). Who is listening to worldly wisdom? People with a worldly mentality listen to everything these systems teach. The world controls society. The world controls social values and people mimic social leaders. Christians should carefully weigh the philosophy of world leaders. Paul said, "Be transformed by the renewing of your mind and don't follow the wisdom of this world." A fine line divides spiritual wisdom and the knowledge that leads to things of the world. "We are of God. He who knows God hears us" (I John 4:6). John made no apology. He said if people are filled with God's Spirit, they will hear God's prophets and apostles.

Listening to the right voice activates faith. We must distinguish between the Word of God from those whom God has called and the words of the world. Some people have more confidence in their paper boys than their pastors. They have more trust in department stores than the church. They will pay a thousand dollars for an item believing that it will be delivered. A man of God can say to them, "God said for me to tell you to stand on your feet and be healed! God will deliver you if you'll walk in faith." They go away saying, "I wonder whether that is really going to happen."

I could weep over the needless suffering and devastating circumstances that occur because people listen to the world and its systems instead of listening to God.

The acceptance of truth or error is determined by whose voice we hear. Truth or error cannot even be judged by what we do. Often we judge people by their actions. God's Word says that judgment is by whom we hear, whom we listen to. Do we listen to worldly politicians? Do we listen to humanistic governmental officials? Are we listening to warmongers or fearmongers?

Or do we listen to what God is saying? The world says, "Your security is in your savings account." God says, "Lay up treasures in heaven." Whom do we hear? Where are our treasures? How much do we invest in the Kingdom of God? How much are we planting into the Kingdom of God? How much do we practice the seed principle? We talk a good game, but where are our treasures? The world says security is in possessions and success. God says that our security is in our relationship with Him.

For years I have ministered to people who are dying. I have held their hands as their last breath is drawn. I receive a call, and a lonely voice says, "Pastor, the end is very near." In that moment between heaven and earth, dying people do not care what kind of house they lived in or what kind of car they drove. The only issue that is important is whether their hearts are right with God.

The spirit of truth and error is determined by our hearing. When we listen to people criticize the cause of God, we open ourselves to the spirit of error. Refuse to listen to anything that pollutes the spirit. Be strong enough to say, "I don't want to hear that." God hated murmuring and complaining more than anything else in the Old Testament. He hates those who sow discord among brethren. Many illnesses in our bodies would be cured immediately if we listened only to truth.

God said, "Test the spirits." The spirit of antichrist will deny the incarnation of Jesus Christ within people in the Church. That spirit denies that God is in the flesh. God is saying, "I have spiritual men and women as earthen vessels and instruments who do My work."

God is not personally in the world, but He empowers ambassadors. Christ Himself ordained the plan. He said, "Listen to them. Hear My servants." The world has always killed men of God because they detest hearing truth. They want to worship the gods of this world. The world says, "Have a good time! Live it up! Do your own thing!" Through the ministry of God's apostles, prophets, evangelists, pastors and teachers, we are instructed to find the will of God by following the spirit of life.

The witness of God must become greater than the witness of man. What if a doctor tells someone that he is going to die in five months? Is that news the witness of man or God? The witness of God is greater than the witness of men. "If we receive the witness of men, the witness of God is greater; for this is the witness of God which He has testified of His Son" (I John 5:9). The witness on the earth is the "called-out" spirit, those who have been called and sent forth by the Lord. The Word has been written by the Spirit. The blood of Jesus Christ and the glorious plan of redemption are both witnesses on planet earth. Hear God's witness on the earth. The witness of men is something totally different. Man will speak about earthquakes, famines and the faltering economy. They will try to diagnose our problems. This is a world of diagnosis and dialogue.

God's witness is greater than the witness of man. God places two types of gifts in the church. First, God gave nine gifts of the Spirit to insure the work of the Holy Spirit and the witness of God (I Corinthians

12:4-11).

Gifts of revelation include wisdom, knowledge and discernment. These are the gifts through which God speaks to His people. Are we going to listen to God or the world? The power gifts of the Spirit are faith, healing and miracles.

Three gifts of inspiration are prophecy, tongues and interpretation. Do we listen to prophecy God gives us? Are we appreciative of gifts of tongues and interpretation? Does that become the witness of God to us? He said, "The Spirit bears witness on the earth. Obey what the Spirit says."

The gifts of the Spirit are given to edify, exhort and comfort (I Corinthians 14:3). The spirit of prophecy may come upon a congregation because the Holy Spirit is in charge. The Holy Spirit distributes these gifts as He wills. Any one of the gifts can be used through Spirit-filled people, but some are more operative within some people than others. Some people have the gift of discernment or wisdom, but the Holy Spirit can use anyone at any given time to manifest His gifts.

The extent of any gift can be explained by the illustration that most people can talk, but some of us have "the gift of gab." By the Spirit, all of us at times have a sense of discernment. We say to someone, "I know something is wrong there." We may never speak of some problem, but we have evidence of the Spirit warning us to be careful. Others may have a continuing gift of discernment. They open themselves to the Spirit, and God uses that gift consistently in ministry. The gifts are the work of the Holy Spirit and function in the church to bring exhortation, edification and comfort.

Immediately after Christ overcame the work of Satan, He assigned ambassadors. He said, "I will give the Church the gift of men and women. I will call them apostles, prophets, evangelists, pastors and teachers" (Ephesians 4:11-12). Their purpose is for the unity of faith, the equipping of the saints and bringing the Church to the image of Christ. These ministries stabilize the Body of Christ. Although any of the gifts may work through the five-fold ministries, ministry is a gift itself. Many people never learn the difference between the gifts of the Spirit and the gifts of ministries.

While the gift of wisdom may speak of things to come, prophetic spirits whom God calls are permitted to discern the day in which they live. Prophets project certain events which will take place.

Learn to listen and be motivated and directed by the Holy Spirit. The Holy Spirit will direct through the gifts of the Spirit as well as through those who are called by God for the purpose of giving direction. Many people can remain spiritually immature because they don't know how to listen to God.

We have the written Word because of the living Word, Jesus Christ, but we also listen to ambassadors whom God sends. We know ministries by their fruit. By opening ourselves to the Spirit of God, truth will penetrate our spirits with God's vision.

For everything that is genuine, Satan produces a counterfeit. Before the real comes, Satan usually begins a counterfeit to bring the real into question. For example, God gives a true gift of wisdom. When the gift of wisdom comes upon us, we visualize a larger panoramic view than the natural mind can see. Satan uses witches and sorcery to reveal many of the same things that one with the gift of wisdom will know. Witches are the counterfeit of the real gift from God.

A counterfeit of the word of knowledge is palm reading. Palm readers can tell certain true things because of familiar spirits working within them. They have knowledge and just enough ability to deceive people because they are ambassadors of Satan. Satan is not omniscient, but he knows many things. Sometimes he knows us better than we know ourselves. He knows exactly where to make us falter. He knows our nature and the weak places in our lives and uses that knowledge to bring us into certain circumstances of testing.

I believe medicine and religion should be in unity. I believe a true merging of psychology and religion should occur. I thank God for merging true science with truths of God. Much of the research into the minds of men and many psychological principles are only humanism. Sometimes psychiatrists and psychologists find weaknesses and address them according to their views of humanity. Dozens of men have come to me for counseling who have been told by psychologists and psychiatrists they would have nervous breakdowns if they tried to alter a gay lifestyle. These doctors tell them to live where they can activate that lifestyle. Peace comes temporarily because they are following their own desires, but that lifestyle never brings God's solution to the problem.

Faith is not the same as positive believing. Positive believing is not necessarily built on a foundation of faith in God. The simplistic strategy of positive thinking can be a prostitution of true faith. Miracles cannot occur by simply activitating positive thoughts. When God's man, Moses, went before Pharaoh, he threw down his rod and the rod became a snake. Then the magicians did exactly the same thing. The snake that God put down swallowed their snake. God says, "For every counterfeit, I have a genuine that will swallow it."

One of God's gifts is genuine healing, but healing cults reside all over the world. Some Christians are even doing cult-like things in the name of Jesus. I heard a man in this city say, "I've been in a room praying for several days. I have saturated my shirt with perspiration and have torn it up into little pieces. Write me at this radio address, send me an offering of 'X' number of dollars, and I will send you a piece of my shirt. Put it on the pillow of your husband and he'll be saved." That faith is not God's gift—it is cult-like. Sand from the Dead Sea, pieces of wood supposedly from the cross and drops of oil from trees in Jerusalem will not bring healing. Healing will come only by the power of the Holy Spirit through the blood of Jesus Christ.

The opposite of prophecy is divination. The woman from Philippi followed Paul saying, "This man is of the Most High God." She had a spirit of divination. Many people don't know the difference between prophecy and divination. They go through life controlled by religious spirits. They think they are hearing from God because they hear voices instructing them. Some people who have religious spirits think they do God's will by killing someone. These "religious" people are driven by spirits of divination. We must know the difference between true voices of prophecy and voices of divination. Divination even comes across pulpits in our day.

All tongues are not of God. Some tongues are spoken from the flesh mind. A few "odd" words in a service do not necessarily mean that the Holy Spirit is speaking. That deception fills many churches. Tongues are legitimate when our spirits are right. When our spirits are pure before God and we don't know how to pray, the Spirit intercedes for us. Through the Spirit language we go beyond our intellects, knowledge and natural abilities to understand. Tongues then become a legitimate means of communication. Why sing in tongues when our native tongues give adequate expressions of praise? Tongues are necessary when we reach a point beyond knowing how to pray. Spirit-filled Christians have so prostituted this gift that we look ridiculous before the world. When the Spirit of God within us says that the situation is beyond knowing how to pray with understanding, we should pray in the Spirit. But we must pray within the Father's will. Jesus' flesh cried, "Let this cup pass from Me," but in the Spirit, He said, "Not My will, but Yours be done."

Most Charismatic circles have never learned to discern spiritual counterfeits. The Church is unstable because Christians have never exercised discernment. They have never learned the difference between "positional authority" and "spiritual authority." As long as the Church doesn't know the difference, Jesus Christ cannot come back. On the basis of the Word of God, Jesus is held in the heavens until the restitution or restoration of all things. He is held in the heavens until we come to that maturity.

How do we begin to demonstrate the Kingdom of God? What is the starting point? The story of the woman with the issue of blood is like many of us. She had heard reports from the doctors that all was hopeless. When she had spent all her money on physicians' and psychiatrists' diagnoses; when she had listened repeatedly to scientific minds, someone said to her, "A young prophet is moving through the land. People are being healed by Him." Her spirit was quickened as she heard those words. Faith begins by hearing. She heard about a prophet in the land and her vision came alive. She saw herself touching Him. She said in her heart, her imagination, her spirit, "If I touch Him, I am going to get well."

Her vision became so strong that she ran to look for Him. Vision must be activated, and when it becomes strong enough, it will take us to the source. When she arrived at the source, she said, "I am the one who received the virtue flowing from you, Jesus." I believe that until she spoke, no metaphysical change occurred whatsoever. But in that moment when Jesus said, "Who touched me?" she said, "It was I." When her voice began to articulate faith, her body began to respond to her spirit. Jesus said something very interesting. He said, "Woman, your faith has made you whole."

The concepts of redemption of the body, overcoming the strong man of this world and pulling him from his throne are important to God's plan for us. We make the decision whether we will be victorious or whether we will allow Satan to control us by disobedience and greediness. God can activate faith in us when we come by obedience to give our lives into His hands.

We must experience a tremendous desire with a proper motivation before God will hear the desires of our hearts. Our desires must be according to God's intentions and will for us. Hannah desired a son. Hannah faced great opposition. People ridiculed her. When one moves with God, he will hear laughter because of his goals. Hannah's husband became an opposing comforter. He offered her an alternative.

Satan always provides alternatives, but there is no substitute for God's way. There is a way that seems right, but the end of that way will lead to the death of God's will. Hannah's husband said to her, "Why is your heart grieved? Am I not better to you than ten sons?" People will come to us with alternatives that will cause disunity in the Body of Christ. Dissimulation causes the Church to have no authority or power.

Hannah prayed at the place where the gift source resided. She went to Eli who was God's representative. One may say, "I don't need God's representative. I can pray and seek God all by myself." God will never answer anyone who circumvents His appointed authority. Why would God tell us to obey those over us

135

in the Lord and then not honor His own Word? Since the Reformation, we have been frightened that the Church will have too much authority. The problem today is that the Church has no authority. Hannah went to the source. She found God's authority in the prophet, Eli, and received the gift that she needed. We sometimes fast and pray when we really need to go to our spiritual authority and listen to God's voice through them.

Eli said to her, "Woman, you shouldn't be drinking like this. Drunkenness is not going to solve your problems." She looked at him with tears streaming down her face, and said, "Oh, man of God, I am not drunk as you think I am. I long for a child."

Hannah prayed in bitterness of soul, and she wept in anguish. Hannah made a vow. Before we get anything from God, we must make a covenant. Some people who are not even tithing expect prosperity. That thinking makes a joke of God. Without being in covenant with God, no results can possibly occur. "Then she made a vow, 'O Lord of hosts, if you will indeed look on the afflictions of your maidservant and remember me, and not forget your maidservant, but will give your maidservant a male child, then I will give him to the Lord all the days of his life, and no razor shall come upon his head' " (I Samuel 1:11).

While she was praying, Eli watched Hannah begin to visualize her promise in her spirit. She began in anguish, but then she reached beyond visualization to a heart experience. Until that time, Hannah had been speaking out of complaint. Eli said, "Go in peace, and the God of Israel grant your petition which you have asked of Him." Hannah put an end to the complaining spirit. She poured her soul out to God and reached a new dimension of faith. Her petition became a vow to God.

We must be diligent in our covenant with God. When Hannah became serious, the man of God gave her a word which she accepted. If we don't accept a word from the Lord when it comes, that promise will never happen. The reason for a drought of miracles in the Church is that people are not hearing and receiving God's promises. If a word of God is spoken, we should act as if it were already done. Faith accepts promises as though they are reality even though they are not yet seen. Faith has a vision of truth and accepts God's provisions to such a degree that finally the vision is activated and becomes a reality.

Because of Hannah's obedience to the covenant that she made, Samuel was born. Hannah believed in her heart, accepted the word of the man of God, and her desire for a child was fulfilled.

The Bible says that until Samuel came, no open revelation had been spoken in Israel. God's Church today is waiting to hear from God, but we must have some Hannah's among us. We need women of faith like the woman with the issue of blood. We must have Anna's who understand their covenants with God until He activates His will upon the earth through open revelation.

I have often wondered of whom God will say in eternity, "Here is one who received a prophet in the name of a prophet. Here is one who took it upon herself or himself to stay before My face for this ministry." Without people who intercede for my ministry, my efforts would fail. My calling would become inactive, passive and worthless. A release of ministry demands true intercession!

We bind "the strong man" so that the power of this world will be judged. The Holy Spirit brings the gifts of the Spirit through the "The Jerusalem Experience." The experience of the Holy Spirit baptism releases gift ministries to the Church. Hear God's ambassadors. In our unity and love, God can activate His power to restore among us.

Without the anointing of the Holy Spirit, sermons are lifeless words. But if we receive God's anointing, we will achieve a new spiritual dimension. The Spirit of God is beginning to correct His Body. We are beginning to discern spirits and understand where the needs are in the Body of Christ. Authoritative voices are crying out, but all is futile without God's anointing.

8

REGROUPING

This is a prophecy: The Church is entering into new arenas of battle. There will be dimensions of warfare unlike anything we've known before. The warfare will not be widespread or widely known, but the battles will occur in strategic areas of ministry, particularly in the minds of influential leaders in the Church.

Immediately after the early Church came into one accord, they received tremendous empowering from the Holy Spirit. They also encountered tremendous conflicts.

Therefore whoever hears these sayings of Mine, and does them, I will liken him to a wise man who built his house on the rock: and the rain descended, the floods came, and the winds blew and beat on that house; and it did not fall, for it was founded on the rock. Now everyone who hears these sayings of Mine, and does not do them will be like a foolish man who built his house on the sand: and the rain descended, the floods came, and the winds blew and beat on that house; and it fell. And great was its fall. (Matthew 7:24-27).

The foundations of our spiritual houses determine whether we can stand through testing. Rain will come and winds will blow. Surviving storms of life does not necessarily depend on the gravity of the storm. Endurance is an indication of the foundation of our lives. Theories and ideas won't work in surviving storms. The simplest excuse for failure is to say, "We didn't have faith," which may not be the case at all. Sometimes it takes more faith to go through the storm than to stop it. Sometimes it takes more faith to go through a fiery furnace than not to go into the furnace at all. The words of Shadrach, Meshach and Abednego were, "Our God is able." God knows what He is doing. If His will does not concur with our plans, then let God's plan be the one that we pursue.

The early Church had a glorious victory. With every victory, Satan tries to bring conflict. Conflict will always occur when we walk by the Spirit. After the glorious, victorious experience in the Upper Room, Peter preached and thousands of people were converted. The disciples immediately went to the temple to pray and magnify the Lord. They saw a lame man by the gate called "Beautiful," and they were filled with compassion. They had a new sense of authority and power with God. When the man reached out with his cup begging for alms, Peter said, "Silver and gold have I none, but such as I have, I'll give to you." They used power and authority with God, taking the man by his hands and lifting him to his feet. As he was lifted, strength came into his ankle bones.

After being lame for forty years, the man was healed. One would think that everyone would be happy about that healing. Not so! Everyone does not rejoice when we prosper. People love us when we are sick, bothered or defeated. When prosperity comes and great things are accomplished for the Lord, we usually encounter jealousy. The foundation of our lives must be so strong that whether we have prosperity or adversity, our houses are secure.

Following the healing of the lame man, the apostles were arrested. Imagine being arrested for healing someone! The frustration of imprisonment for doing good could have been devastating. Their character was undoubtedly questioned because of their arrests. This same attitude is beginning to attack the foundation of life in America. Burdens are imposed upon Christian institutions because of tremendous legal opposition.

Battles continue in great denominations. I have tremendous respect for the Baptist denomination, but when headlines reveal battles between the liberals and conservatives in God's Church, the world enjoys the conflicts. People spend millions of dollars to influence votes for certain issues. The world just sits back and rejoices at seeing turmoil within the Church.

I don't intend to make this a critical issue, but I do intend to speak prophetically. Until the Church ends its inner fighting and refuses to allow the world to see its conflicts, we will never become the standard that God must have in the world.

Church matters must be resolved behind closed doors. Issues need to be discussed openly among us as the early Church did (recorded in Acts 15). We must reach conclusions on important issues so that we can face the world as a unified body: one body, one Lord, one baptism. When the world sees the Church in disarray, they disregard its authority because they perceive it as devouring itself.

Whether one's doctrines are liberal or conservative is not the issue. The issues are not based on appearances or methods of worship. The primary issue is Jesus Christ as the chief cornerstone.

After the apostles were imprisoned, officials didn't quite know how to relate to the men of God because they still praised and magnified the Lord. Then the officials decided to threaten them. When Satan can't do anything else to stop God's children, he roars at them. The devil is cunning. He hides himself, then roars at us. The Bible does not say that the devil is a lion, but rather that the devil goes about "as a roaring lion." Satan should know his game plan was defeated at the cross, but but he just won't give up.

When Peter was arrested and threatened, he said, "I hear your threats, but whom shall we obey? Shall we listen to you or to God? Shall we obey God or man?"

The Bible says that after the officials threatened the apostles, they released them. The Church got together again, still in one accord, and shared together what had happened. They regrouped. A time always comes when we must learn how to regroup. Sometimes regrouping is a very personal thing. Someone once said, "The only difference between a winner and a loser is that a winner fights one more round." When we quit fighting, defeat will surely come. We must never give up or give in to the devil's roar. We must know who we are—what God has called us to do. We must realize that we are on the winning side.

"Now, Lord, look on their threats, and grant to Your servants that with all boldness they may speak Your word, by stretching out Your hand to heal, and that signs and wonders may be done through the name of Your holy Servant Jesus." And when they had prayed, the place where they were assembled together was shaken; and they were all filled with the Holy Spirit, and they spoke the word of God with boldness. (Acts 4:29-31)

"And when they had prayed . . . " Too often the Church has overlooked that important step. We want to move on to the next spiritual plateau, the source of victory.

The early Church had a regrouping experience. They sensed that they were still together and God continued leading them. They left that room with a fresh enduement of power, boldness and God's authority. Everyday we perform certain physical aspects of communion with God. We accept the necessity of that communion—sacrifices of praise. It is rather shameful that sometimes we become weary with repetition of daily, spiritual disciplines.

How should we regroup following a personal calamity such as divorce, death or financial failure? Do we give up by saying it is no use trying to fulfill God's purposes for our lives? We must say, "God, You are still God. You are still on Your throne. I still love You, and You still love me. I may have made mistakes, but I repent this moment of my mistakes. All have sinned and come short of the glory of God. God, I am going to learn by these mistakes and proclaim that Jesus Christ is still Lord of my circumstances."

The first step in regrouping is to examine our foundational truths. People must be willing to examine the truths on which they have built their lives. Theories and doctrines are merely conjecture unless they are founded in truth. Theories are ideas being formalized. Truth is a solid foundation. I have asked God to specify foundational truths that He wants us to build upon.

First, sacramental areas are held in mystery. We have theories and doctrines, but many aspects of faith are still held in mystery. Without apology, I admit that I do not know the mysteries concerning death. All I know is that Paul said, "To be absent from the body is to be present with the Lord."

The Bible says the rich man died and immediately, in hell, he lifted up his eyes. The judgment of the saint and sinner evidently takes place immediately. In direct contrast, Paul said to the Christian, "To be absent from the body is to be present with the Lord." When a Christian dies, I believe two things take place. People near death talk about lights, and almost inevitably they will talk about seeing departed saints and knowing the presence of the Lord.

What is heaven? Heaven means the presence of God and total communication with Him. We get into unimportant theories, doctrines and arguments. The important issue is living with absolute dedication to Jesus Christ and knowing how to confess sin. I do not mean we live in a sinful lifestyle, but we must be confessing overcomers. "Walk in the light as He is in the light and the blood of Jesus Christ continues to cleanse us from all sin." Sin must be confessed. Repent of sin, then go on with the Lord. Do not linger upon sins of the past by continuously reconfessing them. The blood of Jesus Christ is not weak. Once we have confessed sin, we need to go on to some new challenge, some glorious accomplishment for God.

Every believer has the same accessibility to God as an apostle or prophet. God does not give everyone the same calling, but we all have identical access to Him. I believe in the priesthood of all believers. I do not believe in the equal callings from God to all believers. God works with us according to our gifts, potential and openness to Him.

What is the difference in "a truth" and "a doctrine"? A "doctrine" means we continue studying the subject to gain further enlightenment. A "truth" is absolutely immutable, never changing. Jesus Christ is the same yesterday, today and forever. Theories and doctrines change or modify, but truth never changes.

God's love is an eternal truth. Life can be built upon that truth. The character of God never changes. The Apostle Paul concluded I Corinthians 13 with this simple statement, "Now abide faith, hope and love." These are continuing truths that God gives to us. Faith, hope and love last as long as God lasts. That is truth! We can build our lives on faith, hope and love.

Truth in God's Word never depends upon translations. When God speaks, there is no question that His Word is truth. We spend our time debating translations. What are we really doing? We are wasting our time! The truth is in God's Word, absolute truth, and if we find truth, we can build our lives on it. When we come to understand that principle, we take the sword out of Satan's hand.

Jesus is the Christ. Jesus paid the price for us. He is our advocate, our mediator. Everything we need we have by faith in Him. Although we may not live up to His standard with total commitment at all times, He becomes the propitiation for our sins.

When the people brought a sacrifice for their sins in the Old Testament, they never looked at the sins or at the one bringing the sacrifice. They examined the lamb to see if it were spotless. We are the sinners. We are the ones who fall short, but Christ is the sacrifice. God does not look at us as sinners, He looks at the sacrifice we bring—our sacrifices of praise to the Lord, our sacrifices of love for the Lord. We sometimes think that we are examined for our own perfection. No, Jesus is the sacrifice, the spotless one. If our faith is in Him, we take the sword out of the devil's hand. Learning to wage combat

146

is so important. We can stand up and point the devil to the sacrifice that never lies, has never lost a battle, is totally pure, and provides our covering and our salvation.

After the disciples healed the lame man, they were imprisoned and then released. They went back to the basic foundational truths of prayer and fellowship. As they prayed, the place was shaken. The mighty Spirit of God fell among them and rekindled their boldness.

We must regroup ourselves. Let's move toward the promised land. The promised land lies where it has always been. God's promises are the same today as always. We still sit on the outskirts of the promised land. By the grace and help of God, we will eventually take the land promised to us.

Moses talked with God and always seemed to have answers for the people's questions. Joshua was second in command and he would ask Moses what God had said. When Moses died, Joshua was totally confused and uncertain and wondered what they were going to do now that Moses, God's spokesman, had died. Joshua heard the thundering voice of God and received His instructions on how to lead Israel. A time always comes when some things must be buried. When "a Moses" dies, God always has "a Joshua" somewhere.

What is waiting for us on the other side of Jordan? On the other side of Jordan is Jericho which represents walls, a formidable enemy. Jericho shows us that even after we cross over the Jordan, giants must still be confronted. God is pressing us toward the promised land. Like Joshua and the apostles, we must organize and regroup for the battle ahead. We must be in covenant with God today. Some people always shout over past victories. Our accomplishments today measure our spirituality. We become fruitless by dwelling on past victories.

We must learn to truly worship. We must pray as individuals, "God, I want to get in touch with You in my spirit today." Worship recognizes our inadequacies. In worship we have the ability to say, "Lord, I am an empty, broken vessel." God stirs within us the spirit which was in Jeremiah when the vessel was broken and remade. Worship releases that aroma coming out of brokenness. We say, "Lord, out of my broken life, out of my nothingness, receive Your glory."

An able-bodied person running a race is not extraordinary, but when someone runs who is not physically strong, that effort is impressive. I used to be on a track team in college. I ran in the Southeastern Conference, but I was never greatly impressed with winners. I did my share of winning and I thank the Lord for those experiences, but I was not that impressed with winning a race. I saw many runners participate on track teams who did not have great ability. I remember one particular race when everyone finished except one poor runner. He was totally lapped. He was a quarter of a mile behind the others and everyone expected the man to quit his race, but he refused to quit. Another event could not even begin because that runner intended to finish the race. That poor boy kept on running, right by himself. On the last lap he finally staggered across the finish line. People stood up, applauding wildly because he had won his race. He did not win the competitive race, but he won "his" race.

Forget about people who seem to be out ahead and simply say, "God, I am going to win **my** race for You." That is true worship. No matter what age we are, or what our circumstances may be, we can win. The reason we lose muscle is because we don't exercise it.

Worship may be giving God the best effort we have by saying, "God, it is Yours." Worship is a little boy bringing two fish and five loaves of bread to Jesus. Defeat should never enter our mentality. Erase it! Now is the time to regroup and start pressing for the promised land, the Kingdom of God.

Part 3
Operation Unity

9

THE WOMB

When God created His offspring in His own image, He determined that they would bring order and dominion to the earth. God declared the dominion of His Kingdom over everything throughout the entire universe (Genesis 1:26). Lucifer had fallen, causing the universe to need correction. Restoration of creation is essential in every aspect of God's plan. Wrongs in the universe require correction from God.

Adam, God's first offspring, found himself alone. God said, "It is not good that man should be alone." God made a helper for man who could bring healing, restoration and refuge (Genesis 2:18). This helper was created to be a discerner, a teacher, a lover and sometimes even a judge. Woman was created to be an advisor to complete God's plan for man.

God said to Adam, "This is a helper who is both comparable and equal to you" (Genesis 2:18). Eve's appearance was different from Adam's because she was created to be his pleasure. God created her to think as a discerner and advisor to Adam. Women, as God created them, are unique and appealing.

> *Now the serpent was more cunning than any beast of the field which the Lord God had made. And he said to the woman, "Has God indeed said, 'You shall not eat of every tree of the garden'?" And the woman said to the serpent, "We may eat the fruit of the trees of the garden; but of the fruit of the tree which is in the midst of the garden, God has said, 'You shall not eat it, nor shall you touch it, lest you die.'" And the serpent said to the woman, "You will not surely die. For God knows that in the day you eat of it your eyes will be opened, and you will be like God, knowing good and evil." So when the woman saw that the tree was good for food, that it was pleasant to the eyes, and a tree desirable to make one wise, she took of its fruit and ate. She also gave to her husband with her, and he ate. Then the eyes of both of them were opened, and they knew that they were naked; and they sewed fig leaves together and made themselves coverings. (Genesis 3:1-7)*

In their innocence, the man and woman were naked, yet unashamed. Their relationship with God changed after their disobedience.

> *And the Lord God said to the woman, "What is this you have done?" And the woman said, "The serpent deceived me, and I ate." So the Lord God said to the serpent: "Because you have done this, you are cursed more than all*

cattle, and more than every beast of the field; on your belly you shall go, and you shall eat dust all the days of your life. And I will put enmity between you and the woman, and between your seed and her Seed. He shall bruise your head, and you shall bruise his heel." To the woman He said: "I will greatly multiply your sorrow and your conception; in pain you shall bring forth children; your desire shall be for your husband, and he shall rule over you." (Genesis 3:13-16)

One woman, Eve, disobeyed the Word of God. Another woman, Mary, said, "Let it be unto me according to Your Word." The comparison between these women reveals a great truth. The garden of disobedience was the result of rejecting God's plan. Sin marked the womb of a disobedient woman, the life she conceived in her womb, and finally, the innermost fiber of mankind. An antidote for disobedience appeared only when a virgin said, "Let Your Word come alive in me."

Now in the sixth month the angel Gabriel was sent by God to a city of Galilee named Nazareth, to a virgin betrothed to a man whose name was Joseph, of the house of David. The virgin's name was Mary. And having come in, the angel said to her, "Rejoice, highly favored one, the Lord is with you; blessed are you among women!" But when she saw him, she was troubled at his saying, and considered what manner of greeting this was. Then the angel said to her, "Do not be afraid, Mary, for you have found favor with God. And behold, you will conceive in your womb and bring forth a Son, and shall call His name JESUS. He will be great, and will be called the Son of the Highest; and the Lord God will give Him the throne of His father David. And He will reign over the house of Jacob forever, and of

His kingdom there will be no end." Then Mary said to the angel, "How can this be, since I do not know a man?" And the angel answered and said to her, "The Holy Spirit will come upon you, and the power of the Highest will over-shadow you; therefore, also, that Holy One who is to be born will be called the Son of God. Now indeed, Elizabeth your relative has also conceived a son in her old age; and this is now the sixth month for her who was called barren. For with God nothing will be impossible." Then Mary said, "Behold the maidservant of the Lord! Let it be to me according to your word." And the angel departed from her. (Luke 1:26-38)

The living Word of God, Jesus Christ, was conceived in the womb of a virgin. The Word became flesh in the God man, Jesus Christ (John 1:1). Likewise, the Word of God must be made flesh in the Church in order for us to bear witness to the Kingdom which God has called us to demonstrate.

The womb became an eternal battleground. The womb has always depicted life. The Bible says, "Out of his belly (heart), those who believe on Jesus, will flow rivers of living water" (John 7:38). Natural conception and birth graphically symbolize God's offspring in His Church. The Church is the womb of God's Kingdom. God wants to quicken His Word, to bring it alive in us, causing us to live by His Word, not by sight or natural understanding.

"God opens and closes the womb" (Exodus 13:2). The Old Testament declares barrenness to be a curse of God. Families who brought forth many children re-joiced in the fruit of the womb. Many scientific studies today reveal that much of our response to life is fashioned in the womb. Personalities are affected by conditions experienced in mothers' wombs during pregnancy. Such research is very interesting because scripture substantiates the conclusions of this research. We are "fashioned in the womb" (Job 31:15). God spoke about Rebekah "carrying two nations" in her womb (Genesis 25:23). She carried the father of the nation of Israel as well as the father of the Arab nation. Nations are established from the womb. "And he was called a transgressor from the womb" (Isaiah 48:8). Isaiah also says of himself in the following chapter that the Lord "formed him in the womb" (Isaiah 49:1). Jeremiah was ordained to be a prophet from His mother's womb (Jeremiah 1:4-5).

The Bible says that when Elizabeth saw Mary, the mother of the Lord, Elizabeth's womb was quickened by the Holy Spirit (Luke 1:41). I believe Christian parents can expect their children to have a spiritual experience from the mother's womb. Of course, God requires a personal conversion at an age of accountability. Salvation is a conscious and deliberate experience. Man's free will determines if he accepts Jesus Christ, but the Bible records truth that we have overlooked. The scriptures indicate "a quickening of the Holy Spirit" in human experience from the mother's womb.

The Church is the womb of God's truth, His Kingdom in the world. Symbolism? Some will dismiss it as that. The fact is that the Church gives birth to reality, the demonstration of God's Word. New Christians are "babes" in Christ whom the Church nurtures through ministries that bring restoration and parental care. God's Church provides care through the gifts of the Spirit and the fruit of the Spirit. In the womb of God's truth, life is continually birthed. The Church has responsibility for providing mature ministries to care for new Christians.

Christians think that "babes in Christ" should act like mature believers. Our youth ministry, *Alpha*, takes young people in the "spiritual womb" stage and develops their potential. Eventually they grow into full fellowship, desiring the meat of God's Word. Some covenant fellowship groups are "womb ministries." Covenant group leaders reach out to people in the conception stage of God's love. New Christians missing intimate "womb" care are not only insecure and neglected, but they can also be aborted.

Babes in Christ must be treated as babes. They should be fed the milk of the Word. They must learn basic principles before they are ready for spiritual meat. When new Christians go to churches teaching anointed revelation, moving mightily in things of God, the womb ministries—Alpha's, Covenant Communities, etc.—must be strong or many babes will be tragically aborted. Unless spiritual "Dads and Moms" take truth and break it down, giving their spiritual children the milk of the Word, revelation "meat" will only choke them. Teachers should learn how to explain truth and show how God's principles fit into daily life and relationships.

The five-fold ministry is given for equipping or maturing the saints in the womb of God. They minister according to God's purposes. Every person's calling is vital to bring nourishment and growth to the body. The five-fold ministry equips believers, making everyone an able minister within his own realm of influence. A newborn baby emerging from its mother's womb is separated when the umbilical cord is cut. Think of training time in young Christians' lives by using a natural analogy. Called leaders teach them "how to hold a glass" and "go to the potty." Eventually we train them to be powerful soldiers.

Too often the Church neglects Christians making a commitment to the Lord. We baptize them in water, then turn them loose saying, "Now be grown." New believers often have flesh problems or relationship problems. Many times we put them under unbearable guilt because of their immaturity. We don't allow them time to grow and learn. To follow the natural analogy, a baby is held in water in its mother's womb. In spiritual terms, a newborn life must live by the water of the Word. After someone is "born again" into new life, spiritual water sustains him.

As a seed is planted in the natural womb to bring forth life, spiritual seed must also be planted in the womb of the Church to produce a harvest. The womb is inactive until a seed is planted. Even when a womb is functional, unless a seed is planted or conceived, that womb cannot bring forth life. The Word of God is a seed in the spiritual womb. Spiritual seed always brings life. As called ministers sow the seed—the Word of God—in people's hearts, the Word comes alive in them.

Satan also sows his seed. Jesus taught a parable

about a good man who sowed seed. The enemy went to his field and sowed tares among the wheat (Matthew 13:25). Someone asks, "Is that happening in the Church today?" Most definitely! The parable of wheat and tares is reality. But Jesus said, "You back off! I alone know how to judge. Don't go in grabbing up the tares. You will pull up some wheat in the process if you do the separating. Wait and let Me do the judging."

God commands His people, "I just want you to plant good seed. Even if others are planting evil or division, don't fret with their crop. That is My job." Our emphasis should be planting the Word of God in the womb so that spiritual seed will bring forth life. No seed can germinate until the Word comes alive through daily comprehension. The womb of the Church is inactive and barren without God's Word. Life only comes when the seed of God's Word is planted and watered.

The Church is described in God's Word as "a bride." Women have tremendous responsibility to properly channel their abilities to influence. God has given women innate powers of persuasion. If that ability to influence is prostituted, a woman becomes as Jezebel was to Ahab. But when a woman learns to walk by the Spirit, she becomes like Esther to the King. Women have tremendous influence on their husbands and children.

Jesus purposely did not allow the influence of His mother beyond a certain point. When Jesus' mother came in a natural relationship saying, "Go in and tell Jesus that I am here," He replied, "Who is my mother? Who are my brethren?" (Mark 3:32-33). Jesus demonstrated principles that we must understand. We cannot allow natural responsibilities to overshadow spiritual relationships.

Some people serve natural relationships to the extent that they limit their spiritual callings. Natural families sometimes limit the ability of someone to do what God called them to do. Some parents eagerly encourage their children on the soccer field, football field or the basketball court, but never have time to develop spiritual relationships with their children. We are so concerned about what we give in natural relationships that we disregard what God can do in spiritual families.

Jesus said that His mother and brothers were "those who do the will of God." That statement reveals a great truth. Mary and Martha were women who also had great influence in Jesus' life. They must have been very close to Him. When He was ministering in a certain place, he received news that Mary and Martha's brother, Lazarus, was very sick. The women immediately wanted to exert influence upon Jesus because of their close relationship to Him. They thought that Jesus should respond immediately to meet their needs. Jesus never reacted to pressures because of natural affections. He knew something spiritual would occur that transcended natural desires and needs. He said, "I know that Lazarus is sick, but we must wait. Let Me do what God says for Me to do."

Proper balance of priority in relating natural relationships with spiritual callings is necessary. Satan can totally destroy spiritual sensitivity in subtle ways. Plans which may seem "good" can prevent our walking spiritual paths which are God's will. The Bible implies that Anna had great influence with God. She prayed in the temple night and day and continually interceded before the Lord. When baby Jesus was brought to the temple, she knew immediately that Jesus was the Messiah (Luke 2:36-38). How much influence do we have in the throne room of God? How much influence do intercessors have before God as they seek the Lord night and day?

Joyce Strader, wife of Karl Strader who is senior pastor of one of the great churches in America, The Carpenter's Home Church in Lakeland, Florida, said, "We have a group of prayer warriors in our church. Before every service, they walk up and down the aisles praying over every seat and pew. They stay before the Lord night and day. They receive little or no recognition from the pulpit, but we all enjoy the fruit of those prayer warriors' diligence. We are opening a prayer tower twenty-four hours a day. We know prayer is the source of our strength."

How much influence do we have before God? How keen is our spiritual sensitivity? Do we want influence and recognition before men or do we want influence before God? Anna had influence with God. Why was Jesus born at a particular time in history? We answer "in the fullness of time." Perhaps Anna was vital to the timing of Jesus' birth. God is waiting to send His Son to a mature Church who is interceding as Anna did.

The Holy Spirit planted the seed in the womb of Mary. The Holy Spirit overshadowed her. That child in

Mary's womb was conceived by the Holy Spirit planting the seed. Natural man did not plant the spiritual Seed. Likewise, the Holy Spirit conceives life in the womb of the Church. The Word comes alive, begins to grow and takes on form. The Holy Spirit moved on the day of Pentecost to exemplify the birthing from the womb of the Church. Jesus said, "I will build my Church and the gates of hell shall not prevail against it." The Church was barren and lifeless until Pentecost. Jesus told them, "Tarry in a chamber in Jerusalem until you be endued with power, until 'the seed is planted'. "

What was the Upper Room experience in Jerusalem? It was the planting of the seed, the Word, by the Holy Spirit into the Church. It was the quickening and bringing alive of the Word which was incarnate in Jesus Christ. That Word became incarnate in the Church.

Jesus was "the firstfruit." Many people don't understand that description of Jesus. "Firstfruit" means many others like Him will follow. Jesus was the firstfruit of God's incarnation, a man living out God's perfect will. Now He says, "I want to inject life by putting the seed of the Holy Spirit in the Church. My people will bring forth life as they become the 'incarnate Word' on planet Earth." I am sure this definition bothers some theologians, but the Church is "the ongoing expression" of God.

The Holy Spirit is responsible for the maturing process. After the seed is planted, the Holy Spirit begins to guide us, lead us and bring us to the milk and the meat of the Word. Jesus said, "Whatever the Spirit says will not be about Himself. He will quicken your minds concerning Me. You will become expressions of God" (see John 16:13).

That definition of "the Pentecostal experience" is not what we have heard in traditional Pentecostal churches. Being born in a Pentecostal family and having a father who was a preacher for sixty years, I am not a novice to these doctrines. Unfortunately, years ago most people heard, "Get the Holy Spirit" and "Speak with tongues." Many Pentecostals sought an "experience" instead of a life of power. A tremendous difference exists between the two.

Warfare accelerates when we receive liberating revelation because Satan does not want God's people to understand truth. We are receptacles of God's power. The Bible explains Elizabeth's conception in her old age by saying, "With God all things are possible." Many people need to hear those words. "Natural" understanding said to Elizabeth, "You are too old to have a baby." But by God's power, life was quickened within her womb. Elizabeth became pregnant by a supernatural intervention in the natural process.

Circumstances cause some people to say, "I can't handle my life." "I can do nothing about my finances." "My relationships are crumbling." "In my natural mind, my circumstances are hopeless." Meanwhile, God is saying, "If the Holy Spirit quickens a spiritual seed within you, start living by faith and not by sight." How do we visualize ourselves in the Spirit? A defeated businessman? A defeated housewife? A defeated teenager? Faith said to Abraham, "You will have seed in your old age." His natural body said, "Impossible!" God searches for spirits in which the Word of God can be quickened and brought to life by those believing impossible promises.

Spiritual quickening can begin wherever we are. It may start in adverse circumstances. Do we believe the evidence of our infirmities more than we believe God's Word? Peter said, "By His stripes you were healed." Do we see ourselves as paupers, indigents? Do we accept a defeatist mentality more than we believe God supplies our needs according to His riches in glory? God not only blesses us with material riches, but also He releases new energies of creativity to bring us into a proper state of prosperity.

How do we allow the Word of God to come alive in us in order to become the incarnate Word of God? How do we live by faith and not by sight? First of all, we act on God's Word, not on circumstances of life. Someone asks, "How do I act on God's Word?" We must learn God's Word in order to know God's will. Knowledge of the Bible is essential. Someone argues, "Well, I don't know how to reach that place." If we do not know how to pray, the Holy Spirit will pray God's will for us (Romans 8). We must bring our wills to Him without reservation.

Spirit-filled people should pray in the Spirit. We often reach places in our lives of not knowing how we should pray. A wife doesn't know whether to pray for her husband a new job which will require extensive travel. Parents don't know whether to pray for their son to get a basketball scholarship which may take him to a world of temptations. By the natural mind we often say, "I know that would be good for him!" The Spirit knows how to lead us. The wrong direction leads to hell. The Spirit knows the mind of God. Jesus always answered, "But the Father said . . ." We can never experience the reality of this principle in our lives until we actually learn "what the Father says." God's Word becomes His seed in the womb of the Church and in our lives.

How do we know the will of God? When we pray in accord with God's heart, we begin to visualize circumstances by the Spirit. We begin to hear truth by the Spirit. What do we usually hear? Often we hear, "I don't think I can make it today." The Bible says, "Faith comes by hearing, and hearing by the Word of God" (Romans 10:17). We usually fail to comprehend the last part of this verse. We fail to get our hearing by the Word of God. We don't listen to what the Spirit is saying. We decide what we want to accomplish by the mind of reason. We live according to natural desires and natural understanding. God's will is always predicated upon this question: What does the Father say?

I understand vicarious suffering which God sometimes allows His chosen vessels to endure. I have preached that truth, and I know what it means to enter into the sufferings of Christ. Suffering in God's will always brings one to a higher spiritual dimension. Sometimes God's will may not be the obvious condition that is taking place. Solutions which we think are best for us might not bring credit to the Kingdom of God.

166

Samson's tragic death brought more glory to God than his life. I understand these principles. I both preach and live them.

If the Lord says to me, "That situation is vicarious suffering. Leave it alone because I am going to receive glory out of suffering," then I willingly back off. But until God speaks directly to my spirit, I am responsible to act upon whatever principle of faith is revealed in God's Word. Revelation of God's Word is what the Father has said. "Every good and perfect gift is from above, and comes down from the Father of lights . . ." (James 1:17). God's Word teaches, "It is My desire that you be healed. It is My desire that you be healthy and have good things in life."

We must be sure God has spoken. We **ask** by the Spirit, **listen** by the Spirit and finally **see** by the Spirit. Once we hear God's direction by the Spirit, we must begin to see by the Spirit. Our natural minds never see things clearly. Positive thinking is a good practice, but it is not the same as being led by the Spirit. I exhort God's people to comprehend their circumstances by faith and by God's Word.

Many years ago, my church purchased property in the suburbs of Atlanta. I walked to the center of six acres where we planned to build a sanctuary. God told me to get down on my knees to pray. He began to show me what He wanted built on that property. I had seen the vision of this work years before in Phoenix, Arizona. God assured me that He would do great things if I began to see His promises by faith. I visualized our first building by faith. I can't truly say that I saw its whole design in every detail, but I saw the first building. I said to my brother, Pastor Don Paulk, "Don, sketch out something that I'll describe to you." First, I saw the building in my spirit. In essence, the first sketch Don drew became that building. The building was first seen in the natural mind, drawn on a piece of paper, then built. I soon began to see the expanded development of our property by the Spirit.

We built a K-Center auditorium under great criticism. In my mind, God showed me where the building belonged. I began to visualize it by the Spirit. I did not want my own ideas to be counterproductive to God's specific directions. I would say, "Let me describe the building I see in my Spirit." When I first visualized the K-Center, I told others that it would be a huge building looking like a barn. I remember describing the building, "God only said for us to cover the people!" As it turned out, the K-Center auditorium looks more like an airplane hangar. People who see it are astonished at the efficiency of the building. The K-Center is not the final auditorium God wants my congregation to build, but we visualized its structure according to God's direction.

My mind doesn't dwell on the K-Center any longer. My spirit already sees another facility God is preparing His people at Chapel Hill Harvester Church to build. In my Spirit, I have already moved beyond the "tangible." I have moved beyond the ninety acres of our present property. I have moved in agreement with some other dreamers and visionaries. We see mighty Kingdom ministry ahead at Chapel Hill Harvester

Church. Until a vision is born in our spirits, it can never become reality.

The Bible says, "Without a vision [revelation], the people perish" (Proverbs 29:18). Some people relegate all visionaries to the past. Visionaries in our generation look out into the future and see impossible dreams by the Spirit. When a vision is in God's mind and God's will, we can begin to claim it by the Spirit. The seed is planted and the womb is quickened to produce life.

Everyone can be a visionary in individual, life situations. What do we see for ourselves by the Spirit next year or the next five years? What do we believe we are becoming by the Spirit? Some people make excuses that they are "already past forty." So what? What does one's age have to do with obeying God's direction? Abraham was an old man, but by faith he first conceived God's promise in his heart. Abraham said, "I am going to have seed." When he looked at the stars in the heavens and the sands of the sea, he heard God say to him, "Abraham, you will have that many descendants." He only had one promised child in his lifetime, but he had faith for an entire nation of heirs.

When God's people grasp faith principles and understand them, some will move to dimensions they never dreamed possible. Our own natural minds limit us by our not understanding who we are in God and how He wants to activate faith.

God said to Abraham, "You are going to be a father." Abraham believed God's promise. He believed God's promise for an heir more than he believed his old age.

Do we believe God's Word about healing more than we believe our sicknesses? Do we believe God's Word about meeting our needs more than we believe our circumstances? Abraham was still an old man! His sexual life had probably been inactive for some time. Perhaps he was past that time in his life, I don't know. But in his heart and mind, Abraham comprehended God's Word by faith.

Until we understand how to activate faith principles, the flesh will always lead the Spirit. When faith principles dominate our natural minds and we begin to follow the Spirit, then God can do great things for us. I am not teaching the "name it and claim it" doctrine. However, we have limited ourselves. We have let the devil limit our faith by giving up too quickly when we are criticized for following God's direction.

We should never give up on something good. Many people gave up on "shepherding" because some Christian leaders made mistakes. The Church disregarded great truths because of scandals associated with the "shepherding" movement. Truth empowers us with ability to move in faith principles to activate our natural minds and bodies.

After we have heard the Word of God and believe it more than we believe our circumstances, then we must judge our actions by Jesus Christ's example. Jesus Christ must become our standard—not other people around us. We see others failing and defeated, but Jesus is the firstfruit, the One to imitate.

Look to Jesus Christ as the example. What did Jesus

Christ do when He needed a boat? He walked on the water. What did Jesus do when He preached to people who were hungry and didn't have anything to eat? He fed them. Judge life situations by Jesus Christ's example. We make excuses for ourselves by saying that He was the Son of God. Jesus Christ did not have one thing available to Him that is unavailable to us. He said, "These things that I do, you will not only do them, you will do greater works" (John 14:12). We ask, "Greater in fact, or greater in scope?" We excuse ourselves. He said, "Whatever I am doing, you will do also."

We find excuses for our lack of faith. Rather than building upon the foundation of Jesus Christ's example, we build doctrines on our mistakes. When we find ourselves making life decisions, we must ask ourselves what Jesus would do. He was controlled by whatever the Father said to Him.

I love people dearly, but I often become discouraged by their excuses. When I say, "Act like a god," I can hear people saying, "There he goes with the theory of 'the manifest sons of God.'" Forget about theories! Forget about doctrine! Just go back to the simple Word of God! We are "little gods," whether we admit it or not. What are "little gods"? A god is someone who has sovereignty. Everyone is sovereign within certain parameters. We are sovereign about where we are going to eat lunch. We are sovereign about our relationships. We can say "yes" or "no." We are sovereign in many areas of life because we are "little gods."

Animals are not sovereign. Animals are driven by their appetites. We can teach animals certain behavior

171

patterns. When they get through doing tricks, we give them something to eat. Either we treat them or we threaten them. Man is a sovereign being. He makes decisions. God has called His Church to live beyond finite comprehension by understanding the mind of faith. The devil has tormented us, but when we start acting like "kings and priests," we will effectively torment Satan.

The people said to Jesus, "You talk about being a King and toward this end You were born. But we have not seen You act like a King." What did Jesus do? He said, "Go into the village opposite you, and immediately you will find a donkey tied, and a colt with her. Loose them and bring them to Me. And if anyone says anything to you, you shall say, 'The Lord has need of them,' and immediately he will send them" (Matthew 21:2-3).

Jesus rode the donkey into Jerusalem. He didn't have a throne, castle or even decent shoes to wear. He had no place to lay His head, yet He rode into town like a king. He demonstrated living above His circumstances. The devil has made us so subservient to doubt and fear that we live like paupers. The Bible says that the truth will set us free. In truth we will become free men in God and begin to think like God thinks, living above our circumstances and moving by faith. God will honor our efforts because we are living by faith principles.

We must allow the Holy Spirit to activate His will in the womb of the Church by inviting Him into our lives. This terminology may seem shocking, but God will never "rape" His people. God's life comes to us only by

172

invitation. Jesus said to the disciples, "In an act of obedience, go to the upper room and invite Him." By an act of our wills, we must release the womb to the Holy Spirit. We must release our faith to activate God's power. His power will come alive and begin to work within us. By an act of the will, we say, "Here I am, Lord. I release myself to you, Holy Spirit. Plant the seed of your Word within me." We live far beneath our opportunities.

Remember the word to Your servant, upon which You have caused me to hope. This is my comfort in my affliction, for Your word has given me life. You are my portion, O Lord; I have said that I would keep Your words. My soul faints for Your salvation, but I hope in Your word. Forever, O Lord, Your word is settled in heaven. (Psalm 119:49-50,57,81,89)

Unless Your law had been my delight, I would then have perished in my affliction. I understand more than the ancients, because I keep Your precepts. Through Your precepts I get understanding; therefore I hate every false way. I am afflicted very much; revive me, O Lord, according to Your word. Accept, I pray, the freewill offerings of my mouth, O Lord, and teach me Your judgments. My life is continually in my hand, yet I do not forget Your law. (Psalms 119:92,100,104,107-109)

We will perish when affliction comes unless we know the Word of God. The Psalmist said that he understood more than the ancients who lived thousands of years before him because he lived on principles of faith. He spoke "freewill offerings" instead of the words of complainers, critics or faultfinders. If the desires of our hearts are in keeping with God's Word, we should begin

173

to claim them. Life is in our hands! Life is determined by what we do with the Word and how it grows within us. We will become what we hope to be according to our measure of faith.

What are some things we want to happen in the world? What are some promises God wants to birth in our Spirit minds, our faith minds? Where should we plant seeds? We can never receive a spiritual harvest until we plant spiritual seeds. We say that we want family togetherness. We want to stop divorce so that families can remain together. How do we begin? We plant seeds by being sure that relationships are joined by the Lord. "What God has joined together" (Matthew 19:6). We need to be certain that our children are obedient in their conduct. Until we plant seeds in personal relationships, the Church can never live a demonstration of unity and faith.

Unity begins with the seed principle. We activate unity through a covenant relationship with a husband or a wife and our own children. We shouldn't try to bring other Christians into unity of faith when our own families are divided. The Bible asks, "How can one rule in God's spiritual house when he cannot rule his own natural household?" (I Timothy 3:5). I believe Operation Unity throughout the Church will touch the whole world. I know that is thinking "big." That thinking is also "God-like." God said to me, "Operation Unity will touch the world." I believe Him.

Where does Operation Unity begin? It begins in the womb of the Church as individuals allow the seed of God's Word to be quickened in their hearts. God pro-

174

claimed "a year of credibility" for 1985 in my ministry in Atlanta. God said the next year would be "a year of visibility." God never allows visibility until He proves spiritual credibility in the lifestyles of His people. Credibility means genuine unity and love in our households, our churches and within the leadership of a church. Through our obedience God will begin to bring seeds alive which will multiply throughout the world.

Unity must start somewhere! Jesus said to His disciples, "Begin at Jerusalem." The Jerusalem experience was the beginning of a seed principle. He said that He would plant a seed in Jerusalem which would grow and eventually cover the whole world. Operation Unity really began in the upper room on the day of Pentecost. Jesus said, "Stay there until . . ."

Mammon must first be subdued in our own lives. Worldly mammon is defeated first in our own thoughts and actions. Until mammon is overcome in our own homes, it can never be conquered in the household of faith. We play games with mammon's influence. We go around the mountain repeatedly until we deal with mammon in our own thoughts and lives. When our motives are free from mammon, God will cause mammon to fall in the world. Planting the seed in us will bring a harvest that will finally bring the defeat of mammon in the world. Babylon will fall! Worldly systems will fail! We must first plant a seed in the womb of the Church for it to become the standard for the world.

"When He the Holy Ghost has come, He will convict the world of sin" (John 16:8). How will God judge? God will judge the world according to the seed planted in the womb, His church, as it begins to bring forth life. This life sometimes causes growing, tearing and discomfort.

Until a seed is planted and quickened by the Spirit, it can never fulfill God's purposes. A seed dies to itself. Even the natural seed from man dies unless it is integrated and merged to create something other than itself—a new form, a new life. Life comes by an operation of unity in the flesh which God has ordained. Likewise, in the spiritual realm, life begins when the Word of God integrates with one's spirit.

First, hear the Word of God. Then, visualize whatever the Spirit speaks. God's directions will die unless we visualize them. Then, begin to implement His Word. Use whatever resources or tools are at hand. Life can be beautiful if we refuse to feed it with phrases such as "I can't" or "It's too big."

To those who are faced with afflictions, hear the Word of the Lord: Unless God directs you by a holy visitation or prophetic confirmation that He is using your physical body as a vicarious sacrifice to accomplish a great purpose in the Kingdom of God, you should begin to implement God's Word for total healing. Begin to move by faith according to what God has spoken in His Word, not according to advice from the world. Let the principles of God activate life in the physical body.

Kingdom faith never quits. That is the kind of faith God requires of His Church today. It is a faith that activates the womb to bring forth life. We must say, "No matter what the circumstances seem to be, I choose to believe God instead of what I hear and see around me."

10

GOD'S STRUCTURE

The book of Acts indicates that the Church, like the earth at creation, was without structure, formless and void. The Church is defined as a nation. Just as Israel was a nation through which God judged the world, spiritual Israel, God's Church, are the people by whom God will judge the world.

(Now this, "He ascended"—what does it mean but that He also first descended into the lower parts of the earth? He who descended is also the One who ascended far above all the heavens, that He might fill all things.) And He Himself gave some to be apostles, some prophets, some evangelists, and some pastors and teachers, for the equipping of the saints for the work of the ministry, for the edifying

of the body of Christ . . . (Ephesians 4:9-12)

Jesus went to hell and back to establish structure in His Body. He empowered that structure with the Holy Spirit. Israel's religion had been in confusion when Jesus was born. Religion had become mere ritual. Until John the Baptist came, no prophet had spoken God's Word in Israel for approximately four hundred years. After Jesus ascended into heaven, the Spirit of God moved in the upper room. God said, "I will give you power. I will give you structure."

We have misunderstood and abused God's plan for us. We made structure in the Church into positional authority. We chose our own leaders. With "itching ears" Christians have said, "I like the way this man says it." "I like the way this woman says it." People jump from sheepfold to sheepfold without understanding leadership, never realizing that God says, "I put My shepherd at the door. Anyone who tries to go in and out any other way is a liar and a thief" (John 10:1). The Kingdom of God will never come without true shepherds. We must submit our thinking to God's order and design.

The Spirit of the Lord moves to build structure, make assignments, issue callings, and empower the Church with spiritual gifts. Jesus said, "My sheep hear My voice, and I know them, and they follow Me" (John 10:27).

Rebellion is not usually obvious, but enters the Church in subtle ways. Rebellion is simply defined as

180

disobeying the Lord. One can be in rebellion by honoring someone who is second in command to make a point of ignoring the one who is first in command. In essence, a person says to the spiritual leader in a particular church, "I honor the one who is your helper over you." Many people never understand that attitude to be rebellion.

For example, suppose a pastor is leaving a church where he has served with several other pastors as well as a senior pastor. In his farewell remarks he says, "I want to thank the pastors who are here. I want to thank all the members of the Church who helped me." If he does not give any thanks specifically to the senior pastor, he is in rebellion. Why do I contend that he is in rebellion? That man is choosing his own authority. He is choosing to recognize the ones he allows to minister to him.

Rebellion begins with our boys and girls in their early training. If parents don't lovingly teach their households the importance of worship, they will eventually say, "My God, where did I lose them?" Children are lost when they feel intimidated about doing the things of the Lord. When children have no intimidation about serving the Lord, that spiritual freedom usually began by honoring the Lord at home.

On the day of Pentecost, darkness was dispelled. An illumination sat upon the heads of each of the disciples. The Spirit came to dispel darkness. Our world is full of darkness today. In many ways the earth is still formless and void, but the Spirit of God is coming to bring illumination. Pentecost ignites illumination of the

181

Spirit in understanding God's ways. Tongues of fire were symbolic of the inner enlightenment within believers. Jesus Christ is that light. Through the power of the Holy Spirit, all obstruction is removed and we are able to share His light with the world.

Tongues of fire indicated that God's illumination came to enlighten, to place His brand upon our minds. The antichrist will brand foreheads (humanistic thinking), but Christ, through the Holy Spirit, will place His understanding in open hearts and spiritual minds. He will give His people the tools of authority to defeat Satan.

The Church is out of order when God's people propagate songs written by the world and then call them "spiritual songs." We provide music conferences at our church because we have a responsibility to share structure that God has revealed to us concerning true worship. In God's structure, He will always release power and revelation. Pure worship releases revelation from God as all things flow decently and in order.

A song that came indirectly out of the ministry of Chapel Hill, "Upon This Rock," is sung at Baptist churches as well as Pentecostal churches. "Upon This Rock" received the Dove Award as "Song of the Year" in 1985. Songs that are coming from the heart of God are going to receive recognition among spiritual people and bring God's people into unity. God's people are going to get tired of meaningless little ditties that fail to edify their spirits with life and light.

Artists, trying to do religious things, have taken the

gold and silver of God into strange temples. Joel said,
". . . you have taken My silver and My gold, and have
carried into your temples My prized possessions" (Joel
3:5). Some Christian musicians have taken God's gifts
to Nashville to merchandise them. They have taken
God's gifts into strange temples and attempted to
entertain people with songs the world says are "great"
and "wonderful." God is saying, "This gift belongs to
My Church. This talent is a ministry to My Church."

Satan is extremely subtle in his strategy. The song
recorded by a group of artists to feed starving people in
Ethiopia did not mention the name of Jesus Christ. I
didn't say that the song didn't mention "god." I said it
did not mention "Jesus Christ." Satan calls himself "a
god." Many people openly refer to "god," but the Bible
proclaims that Jesus Christ is the chief cornerstone.
Jesus Christ is also the stumbling block.

Musicians who say, "I thank God . . ." can be referring to anything from their pocketbooks to their lusts
for fame. Whenever Jesus is truly acknowledged as the
chief cornerstone, a departure from evil always occurs.
Sinful lifestyles indicate that Christ is a stumbling
block in their spirits. Christ motivates a departure
from evil, or He will become the stumbling stone who
causes eternal separation from God. Jesus is the chief
cornerstone of everything that God blesses.

The foundational Rock of the Kingdom is the revelation of Jesus Christ! Jesus did not say, "I will build my
Church on eschatology [end time theology], theories
about where the antichrist is hiding, or issues causing
divisions in the Church." Jesus never said, "I'm going

183

to build my Church on praise and worship." Many people have made praise into a god. Methods have become gods to many Christian people. Structure and form are meaningless unless they are anointed by the Spirit of God. Jesus didn't say, "I'll build My Church on signs and wonders." He said, "I'll build my Church on the revelation of Who I am."

What did people see at Pentecost?

Now there were dwelling in Jerusalem Jews, devout men, from every nation under heaven. And when this sound occurred, the multitude came together, and were confused, because everyone heard them speak in his own language. Then they were all amazed and marveled, saying to one another, "Look, are not all these who speak Galileans? And how is it that we hear, each in our own language in which we were born? Parthians and Medes and Elamites, those dwelling in Mesopotamia, Judea and Cappadocia, Pontus and Asia, Phrygia and Pamphylia, Egypt and the parts of Libya adjoining Cyrene, visitors from Rome, both Jews and proselytes, Cretans and Arabs—we hear them speaking in our own tongues the wonderful works of God." So they were all amazed and perplexed, saying to one another, "Whatever could this mean?" (Acts 2:5-12)

The Bible says that in the last days men will be fearful. Nations will be perplexed, amazed, wondering what is happening. God is beginning to gather His Church together by His Spirit. He is going to unite them on spiritual principles of unity.

God's people are going to begin to know who their generals are and they will recognize whom to follow. They will understand how to move by the Spirit. God will develop His anointed structure in His army. He will make that which is formless and void to come alive with power. The world is going to ask, "What does this mean? What has happened to Methodists, Baptists and Presbyterians who used to fight each other? They are no longer fighting. They are built on the rock, Jesus Christ. Their songs are no longer songs of the flesh. They are singing together about Jesus Christ, the solid rock. They are singing songs that proclaim the Kingdom, the majesty of God, the worthy Lamb."

But Peter, standing up with the eleven, raised his voice and said to them, "Men of Judea and all who dwell in Jerusalem, let this be known to you, and heed my words. For these are not drunk, as you suppose, since it is only the third hour of the day. But this is what was spoken by the prophet Joel." (Acts 2:14-16)

The earth is entering into judgment as the power of God is being poured out on His people. The Church was born, has endured many trials, has traveled through the wilderness, and now is finally reaching the promised land.

The disciples weren't drunk. They experienced what God said would happen. No one can control a sovereign God. We can never control God's plan and His purposes. People can fight against Him, but the revelation of Jesus Christ will be established and fulfilled in the earth. Individuals, institutions or nations that war against Christ will begin falling apart both structurally and financially. Worldly kingdoms will topple because people must choose to be either for Jesus

Christ or against Him.

The tools of authority begin with the callings of God. Other tools of authority are the gifts of the Spirit. Everything we need to be victorious is available to us. The only reason God's people don't have victory is because we don't use our spiritual tools. Wisdom has always been available to God's people if they are willing to come to the rock. If we fail to find wisdom, it's because we don't go to the source. Discernment has been given by God to the Church. Some believers are given the gift of healing. Churches who refuse to believe in the ministry gifts, who don't believe they are promised in God's Word for the Church today, don't receive those tools of authority. Anyone who understands God's Word and activates it will receive the authority to perform His will.

Ezekiel prophesied the same vision that Joel saw. Prophecy is timeless, revealing God's purposes, disclosing the heart of God to any generation. Ezekiel, a mighty prophet of God, talks about the sins of Jerusalem which God judges.

Now, son of man, will you judge, will you judge the bloody city? Yes, show her all her abominations! Look, the princes of Israel: each one has used his power to shed blood in you. (Ezekiel 22:2,6)

Ezekiel was prophesying to the nation, Israel. Though God raised Israel up as a prototype of the Kingdom, all she did was shed blood. Israel's leaders were wicked. Ezekiel spoke of the judgment against Jerusalem and Samaria.

The Church today is in disarray. No one can identify "the hand" in the Body of Christ. "The feet" of evangelism are almost undefinable. Teachers of the Word are divided by doctrines and traditions. Many Christians fail to recognize all the callings in the five-fold ministry. They don't understand their own callings. The Body is scattered because everyone is dedicated to fulfilling his own plan.

God commanded the prophet, Ezekiel, to prophesy over the bones that lay in the valley. "The hand of the Lord came upon me and brought me out in the Spirit of the Lord, and set me down in the midst of the valley; and it was full of bones" (Ezekiel 37:1). Ezekiel looked at the bones. God asked Him, "Can these bones live?" That is the same question that I ask the Church today, "Can these bones live again? Are these bones too far spent, steeped in formulas and formalism? Are these bones too infiltrated, enmeshed in reason? Has the Church so entangled itself with humanism that she can't be set free? Can these bones live again?"

James Robison shared with me that God quickened his spirit as he read a book I wrote called **The Wounded Body of Christ.** He said, "Earl, our spirits have been joined." God is raising up men who comprehend that the Body of Christ is scattered and wounded. Can these bones live again? Will we say, "Hold it, we have people in positional authority who disagree. We have organizational differences that will stop the bones from living"?

Who will say, "These bones can live again"? How are they going to live? God told Ezekiel, "Prophesy to these

187

bones, and say to them, 'O dry bones, hear the word of the Lord!' " (Ezekiel 37:4). Without the ministry of prophets today, the Spirit of God cannot move over the dry bones of the Church. The Church will live only when we receive the prophetic Word of God.

Well-known men of God recently watched a video of some messages preached at my church in Atlanta on the book of Revelation. They said, "That is the Word of God. I don't care what opposition to that ministry says, the messages are truth!" Those men took the tapes to others and they shared them together. Finally they shared the tapes with their positional overseer. They asked him, "Is this the word of the Lord?" And he answered them, "This is the word of the Lord." Some will hear. Dry bones will come alive. Those bones are going to move together with life. God will have a Church that will follow His sure direction.

". . . Surely I will cause breath to enter into you, and you shall live . . . So I prophesied as I was commanded" (Ezekiel 37:5,7). What a sobering word! Someone says, "I know the weaknesses of that earthen vessel who is prophesying. I know the problems of that man or woman of God." Remember that God put treasures in earthen vessels.

". . . as I prophesied, there was a noise, and suddenly a rattling" (Ezekiel 37:7). In the upper room, "suddenly there came a sound from heaven, as of a rushing mighty wind, and it filled the whole house where they were sitting" (Acts 2:2). The same Spirit who moved on the dry bones moved also at Pentecost. This recorded event applies to the Church today as well. When the

Spirit of God moved at Pentecost, the sound of a mighty rushing wind filled the upper room. The Spirit of God moved on the face of the deep, a place formless and void. The same Spirit of God who shook the old earth at creation is the Spirit making old things new today. Don't ever interfere where the Spirit of God is moving. God's judgment against those who interfere with His plan will be quick and sure.

Then He said to me, "Prophesy to the breath, prophesy, son of man, and say to the breath, 'Thus says the Lord God: "Come from the four winds, O breath, and breathe on these slain, that they may live."' " So I prophesied as He commanded me, and breath came into them, and they lived, and stood upon their feet, an exceedingly great army. Then He said to me, "Son of man, these bones are the whole house of Israel. They indeed say, 'Our bones are dry, our hope is lost, and we ourselves are cut off!' Therefore prophesy and say to them, 'Thus says the Lord God: "Behold, O My people, I will open your graves and cause you to come up from your graves, and bring you into the land of Israel."' " (Ezekiel 37:9-12)

The house of Israel is the household of faith. The Jews say, "We are God's chosen household because we are born to Abraham." But Jesus said, "And do not think to say to yourselves, 'We have Abraham as our father.' For I say to you that God is able to raise up children to Abraham from these stones" (Matthew 3:9).

Stinking, putrefied graves have formalized true worship. God is saying, "I will never move in the Spirit until you come forth out of your graves."

"I will put My Spirit in you, and you shall live, and I

189

will place you in your own land" (Ezekiel 37:14). In the culmination of this prophecy, God says, "I will make them one nation in the land, on the mountains of Israel; and one king shall be king over them all; they shall no longer be two nations, nor shall they ever be divided into two kingdoms again" (Ezekiel 37:22).

The New Jerusalem of God is taking on reality, form and structure. God is waiting for the prophetic Word to release the moving of His Spirit. He is waiting for the bones to come together so that He can judge the sins of the world. He is waiting to move in the authority and structure that He has ordained. God will perform His will swiftly. I don't believe these events will take fifty years. Knowledge concerning the timing of history rests with God alone, but God's Word promises that we will know the seasons. I believe we are in the season of the final generation, and God will move swiftly.

God's Word records that the first thing Peter and John did after the day of Pentecost was to go to the temple. Why? The temple had become an abomination to God. Worship systems were off-center and profane. Peter and John were the seed, the sons of the resurrection. Jesus had purged the temple and reproved the money changers for making it into a "den of thieves," but it also became the responsibility of Peter to reprimand religious leaders who supposedly represented God.

God is forming His worship centers in the world today. The problem yet to be addressed is the proper structure of those worship centers. Many churches still don't even know who is in charge. Too many churches still vote the preacher in, then vote him out. If God says something, they fail to recognize His voice. A pulpit committee called on me recently. I was very courteous to them, but I told them firmly, "God does not call preachers by committee consensus." The problem today is that pulpits are swapped and bargained like corporate positions. Ministries are not even built in visions; they are built on the basis of positions, salaries and parsonages. No wonder Jesus' ministry demonstrated, "Strip Me of everything. I don't even want a place to lay My head. Take your bargaining power away so I won't be under any obligation to you. I will owe no man." Jesus taught about experiences of the heart, visions of the eternal Kingdom.

The Son of God brings everything together when He is allowed His rightful place as the head of the Body. Pentecost is the gift of power to the Church. God's power will enable the Church to become that witness to the world through their callings, gifts and the assembling of the saints in unity.

The assembly of the saints is a mighty force in the world. A true assembly of saints know the voice of their master. They know the voice of the shepherd. They know how to receive and give ministry.

God said to Ezekiel,

"As for you, son of man, the children of your people are talking about you beside the walls and in the doors of the houses; and they speak to one another, everyone saying to his brother, 'Please come and hear what the word is that comes from the Lord.' So they come to you as people do, they sit before you as My people, and they hear your

*words, but they do not do them, for with their mouth they show much love, but their hearts pursue their own gain."
(Ezekiel 33:30-31)*

What a word of the Lord! God's people pursue their own desires. They follow what they want to do for their own purposes. They hear the Word of the Lord, even articulate it, but down deep inside their hearts are rebellious. They want to lead their own little groups. Jesus Christ is the only head. We must recognize His structure and where we fit into that structure.

God recently spoke to me and said, "I have had you in Atlanta for thirty-four years. No one in a major church in this city has ministered longer than you have. The message of the baptism of the Holy Spirit was proclaimed through you on television for many years, crossing denominational lines all over this area. I have put you through the furnace and tried you by fire. Now I find you to be a servant who can open this city to My ministries. I want to show the world how the principle of shepherds in charge of My cities works—not physically or naturally—but spiritually in charge of My cities."

The Lord gave me a term, "Operation Unity," which sounds impossible. Someone says, "How do you know other spiritual leaders will come to Atlanta?" That is not my problem. My problem is doing what God said for me to do. We will open this church to ministries that are built upon the revelation of Jesus. These ministries may not agree with our eschatology, our methods of operation, or our types of worship, but they will agree with us on the revelation that Jesus is the Christ. Jesus said to me, ". . . on that [revelation] I will build my Church, and you will be one of the men whom I will use to proclaim it. You have been proclaiming it. Now I want you to expand that commission."

God is going to breathe on dry bones, and those bones are going to start coming together. They are going to be a mighty army of God. The whole world will see God's Church.

What if others don't respond? That is not my problem. The answer to their response lies in the power of prayer. We need to start praying, "God, we come against every power and principality that would thwart 'Operation Unity' in the Body of Christ."

Operation Unity starts by the movement of the Holy Spirit in us. It starts by the word of prophecy, the anointing of God. When God begins to move, who is going to stop Him? The swift movements of God are about to begin in power. God is creating a standard by which He can judge the whole universe. His offspring are finding out who they are, the source of their authority, and appropriating the power of the Holy Ghost. God's authority, released through God's structure in His Church, can change the whole world.

11

BECOMING HIS PLEASURE

God loves people who are lost. He never despises or forgets them. He still loves them and wants them to come home. When the prodigal son had been touched by the Spirit of God and returned home, his father ordered a great celebration. But while the household celebrated over the son who had been lost, something happened.

Now his older son was in the field. And as he came and drew near to the house, he heard music and dancing. So he called one of the servants and asked what these things meant. And he said to him, "Your brother has come, and because he has received him safe and sound, your father has killed the fatted calf." But he was angry and would not go in. Therefore his father came out and pleaded with him. So he answered and said to his father, "Lo, these many years I have been serving you; I never transgressed your commandment at any time; and yet you never gave me a young goat, that I might make merry with my friends. But as soon as this son of yours came, who has devoured your livelihood with harlots, you killed the fatted calf for him." And he said to him, "Son, you are always with me, and all that I have is yours. It was right that we should make merry and be glad, for your brother was dead and is alive again, and was lost and is found." (Luke 15:25-32)

The father reminded his son that all he possessed had been at his disposal at any time. He could have killed a calf or thrown a party whenever he wanted to.

God told me that the Father's answer to the older brother is where the Church is today. We celebrate with the angels over "prodigals" who come home. That celebration is glorious, but God is saying, "Few people in My house understand who they are. They don't know that they can kill the fatted calf at any time." We sit around complaining, "My, what great gifts God has given to Oral Roberts, T. L. Osborne and Kenneth Copeland." We never stop to realize, "I am a part of this family! I have a right to minister the gifts God has given to me."

Without being presumptuous, I believe that people have a right to be their best for God. The devil has put us into such negative thought patterns that we don't even have confidence in the ministry God has given to us. We spend our time criticizing God's calling in somebody else's ministry instead of claiming our own heritage. "Why didn't God give me that house?" "Why didn't God give me a talent to sing like he does?" All the time God is saying, "You have something to offer my Kingdom. I have given a ministry to you."

The celebration was proper for the one who was lost. But unfortunately, the older son had never activated his desires. "Delight yourself also in the Lord, and He shall give you the desires of your heart" (Psalm 37:4). Many times we have desires in our hearts, but we don't know how to exercise them. We are complete in Jesus Christ. He has already given us many things, yet we stand begging, asking Him for things which He has already provided. How do we recognize and release our gifts for ministry?

For in Him dwells all the fullness of the Godhead bodily; and you are complete in Him, who is the head of all principality and power. (Colossians 2:9-10)

. . . as His divine power has given to us all things that pertain to life and godliness, through the knowledge of Him who called us by glory and virtue, by which have been given to us exceedingly great and precious promises, that through these you may be partakers of the divine nature, having escaped the corruption that is in the world through lust. (II Peter 1:3-4)

All things have been given to us, even to the point of allowing us to share the divine nature of Jesus. Sharing His nature is a definition of the ongoing incarnation of God on the earth. "Christ in us, the hope of glory." His inheritance is already ours. If we found the key to unlock these truths in demonstration, what would happen? What would immediately be ours? He said, "I have already given you all things." He said, "All these things that I do, you shall do." What is the latter part of that verse? "... and greater." Why? "Because I go to the Father, and I am going to be there in intercession for you."

"... If two of you agree on earth concerning anything, it will be done by My Father in heaven" (Matthew 18:19). Built into that promise is fellowship, unity, understanding God's provision, and Christ's power in us. Why aren't we doing it? I know we experience miracles—supernatural intervention—dimensionally, but generally the Church still does not know how "to loose and to bind."

And these signs will follow those who believe: In My name they will cast out demons; they will speak with new tongues; they will take up serpents; and if they drink anything deadly, it will by no means hurt them; they will lay hands on the sick, and they will recover. (Mark 16:17-18)

The next move of God awaits our comprehension and enactment of spiritual authority. The next move of God awaits Christ in us taking dominion, being the standard by which God can judge the world. The next move of God awaits the total oneness of the family of God in heaven and earth. What hinders these three things from happening? If we can demonstrate these things, then Christ can come again!

But their minds were hardened. For until this day the same veil remains unlifted in the reading of the Old Tes-

tament, because the veil is taken away in Christ. But even to this day, when Moses is read, a veil lies on their heart. Nevertheless when one turns to the Lord, the veil is taken away. Now the Lord is the Spirit; and where the Spirit of the Lord is, there is liberty. But we all, with unveiled face, beholding as in a mirror the glory of the Lord, are being transformed into the same image from glory to glory, just as by the Spirit of the Lord. (II Corinthians 3:14-18)

Who is Paul talking about in this passage? He is referring to Israel. The veil remains over their faces. They continue to regard Moses as their authority. When the Spirit of God comes to Israel and she finally accepts Jesus as the Christ, the chief cornerstone, the veil is taken away. Until then, the veil remains. "Liberty" in this passage has nothing to do with dancing in church or lifting our hands in praise to God. Of course freedom in worship is wonderful, but that is not the point Paul is making. "Liberty" contrasts with "the bondage" to Moses and the law. The first hindrance that must be removed is the veil that yet remains over the eyes of Israel. We must pray for Israel's salvation.

Or do you not know, brethren (for I speak to those who know the law), that the law has dominion over a man as long as he lives? For the woman who has a husband is bound by the law to her husband as long as he lives. But if the husband dies, she is released from the law of her husband. So then if, while her husband lives, she marries another man, she will be called an adulteress; but if her husband dies, she is free from that law, so that she is no adulteress, though she has married another man. Therefore, my brethren, you also have become dead to the law through the body of Christ, that you may be married to

199

*another, even to Him who was raised from the dead, that
we should bear fruit to God. For when we were in the flesh,
the passions of sins which were aroused by the law were at
work in our members to bear fruit to death. But now we
have been delivered from the law, having died to what we
were held by, so that we should serve in the newness of the
Spirit and not in the oldness of the letter. (Romans 7:1-6)*

The law of Moses made us realize that we are trans-
gressors. The law must die. If we hold onto the law of
Moses and try to marry Jesus at the same time, we
make Christ a polygamist. A bride who espouses two
covenants is an adulterous woman.

The law made us aware of our guilt. That bittersweet
"no" causes us to want to do whatever has been forbidden. The law increases passion.

Until this veil (the law) is taken away and we admit
Israel's need for salvation through Jesus, God cannot
move again. We must intercede before God concerning
Israel who is lost.

The law produces guilt. Too many Christians go
around under a great cloud of guilt. "Beloved, if our
heart does not condemn us, we have confidence toward
God" (I John 3:21). The law binds us in our conduct. We
are unable to walk in freedom, the Spirit of Christ. We
are held prisoner by a covenant that no longer exists.
We cannot release God's power because we never feel
worthy. We are always saying, "Look at my flesh. Look
at my problems." Isn't it about time Christians said,
"Look at Christ in me! Christ in me has made me a new
creation"?

Holding onto the old covenant under the Mosaic law gives strength to the law. That stubborn grasp is the power of the law; ". . . the strength of sin is the law" (I Corinthians 15:56). The reason we have not entered into the release of God's mighty power is because not only do we hold onto the law, but also we bless people who continue holding onto the law. We bless the nation who says, "We live by the law. Moses is our teacher." We are hindered from accomplishing what we must do for Christ to come again because the veil has not been removed.

Another hindrance is our misunderstanding of prayer. I really had to converse with the Lord about this subject and we had some interesting conversations. When I was only a young preacher, I often preached at campmeetings. I wanted to impress another preacher that I admired so much, Pastor Frank Lemons. He was a man I respected, a sober man who really had an ability to teach the Word of the Lord. We were roommates at a campmeeting, and I thought I had an excellent opportunity to impress him with my ability to pray. No young preacher goes to bed without getting down upon his knees and crying, "Oh, God! My Father! My Father!" And then young preachers tell God what to do! I thought that Brother Frank would show me how it ought to be done. I could impress him with my spirituality at the same time.

I looked over at Pastor Lemons sitting on the side of his bed. He looked back at me like I was some kind of nut! All of a sudden, I saw his mouth moving a little bit like he was talking to someone. Then do you know what

he did? He turned off the light and went to sleep! I
thought, "That man doesn't even have a touch of God
in him! I am spiritual, and he is carnal!" It took me
forty years to learn that the man understood prayer.
Prayer is conversation with God. Christ in us simply
gives a report to the Father. We must constantly, continuously communicate with Him.

> *Where do wars and fights come from among you? Do they*
> *not come from your desires for pleasure that war in your*
> *members? You lust and do not have. You murder and covet*
> *and cannot obtain. You fight and war. Yet you do not have*
> *because you do not ask. You ask and do not receive,*
> *because you ask amiss, that you may spend it on your*
> *pleasures. (James 4:1-3)*

We are known by whose "pleasure" we are and by the
things we do. Lust can never be satisfied. Murmuring
and complaining get us nowhere.

Many people think praying is asking God for something. "God, I need a tall, dark, handsome young man,
twenty-two years old, with a Cadillac and a house with
seven bathrooms." We lust, living as paupers. We do
not receive from God because we ask for our own pleasure. We are made to be the pleasure of God. If we seek
first the Kingdom of God, He will provide abundantly
the things we need. He knows what our needs are.
Apparently, listing our needs is not the reason we pray.

Being "a pleasure" is a key to good relationships and
harmonious family living. Understanding how to be
someone's "pleasure" could solve problems in many
households. If men understood that principle, they

would capture the total interest of their wives and hell couldn't break them loose. Too many husbands and wives regard marriage with a "What am I going to get out of this?" attitude.

Adulterers and adulteresses! Do you not know that friend-ship with the world is enmity with God? Whoever there-fore wants to be a friend of the world makes himself an enemy of God. (James 4:4)

We cannot hang onto the world with one hand and God with the other. It will not work. Dual allegiance is the reason our prayers are not heard or answered.

Learning how to be the pleasure of God; learning how to converse constantly with the Christ in us will bring Christ back again. I believe God goes shopping with us, to school with us, on dates with us. I do not know quite how far we take Him with us, but He is willing to go! Sometimes He probably backs off and says, "Well, I'll just let you do that. I will go over here and find somebody who wants to do things I want to do." I do not expect that to be a popular statement, but it is truth. If Christ controls us, we will never go any-where that Christ would not go. We will not enjoy a meal at any table where He is not welcome. We won't fellowship anywhere that Christ would be rejected. Compromise is the reason many prayers are unan-swered. People take Christ to the wrong places and force Him to walk away. They scream and cry like He is far away when actually they left Him behind. Christ is not far away. A whisper calls His attention when one is in covenant with Him.

"Jesus, You are here with me. Wherever I go, You can go. I love you every morning, noon and night." When one is in covenant with the Lord, Jesus even helps with shopping. We pray, "I would like to get that video recorder if that seems good with you." And the Lord will say, "Well, okay, but just hang around awhile and prices will go down. I will tell you when to buy one." Christ has more sense than we do! If we listen to Him, we will be amazed at what He will tell us. We will be astonished at how much He knows! The word "Emmanuel" means "Christ in us." We sing it, especially at Christmas time, yet often we do not even know or experience its meaning.

Elijah mocked the prophets of Baal saying, "Cry aloud, for he is a god; either he is meditating, or he is busy, or he is on a journey, or perhaps he is sleeping and must be awakened" (I Kings 18:27). The prophets of Baal reacted exactly as Elijah said. They screamed louder and louder. They cut themselves, blood gushing from their bodies. Some Christians may be shocked to learn that God is not deaf. We can whisper to Him. As a matter of fact, the more intimate we become with Him, the quieter our conversations will be. Imagine how a young lady would react if her boyfriend shouted in her face, "HONEY, I LOVE YOU!" The poor girl would be deaf for a month. Instead he gets close to her and whispers, "Oh, you are so pretty! You are the most adorable woman I have ever known!"

But in our intimacy with God, we think we have to be loud. We think we have to repeat everything continuously. We say, "Jesus, I really need a wife. Oh, Jesus, I do need a wife. Do You know that I need a wife, Jesus? Just one wife will do, Lord. Just one wife." And God says, "Do you think I am a fool? I heard you the first time!" We are not to be like the heathen who pray vain repetitions (Matthew 6:7).

The widow kept coming to the unrighteous judge. We have used that parable to understand prayer, but I discovered that parable has nothing to do with repetitious prayers at all (Luke 18:5). To get the total understanding of that parable, one must go back to the seventeenth chapter of Luke. The parable refers to the coming of the Lord, the coming of the Kingdom. "Now when He was asked by the Pharisees when the kingdom of God would come, He answered them and said, 'The kingdom of God does not come with observation'" (Luke 17:20). He describes two people in the field; one is left and one is taken (Luke 17:36). Jesus is talking about the coming of His Kingdom. Then He continues this lesson by giving a parable concerning the second coming.

> *Then He spoke a parable to them, that men always ought to pray and not lose heart, saying: "There was in a certain city a judge who did not fear God nor regard man. Now there was a widow in that city; and she came to him, saying, 'Avenge me of my adversary.' And he would not for a while; but afterward he said within himself, 'Though I do not fear God nor regard man, yet because this widow troubles me I will avenge her, lest by her continual coming she weary me.'" (Luke 18:1-5)*

Jesus is giving an example to illustrate intercession for the Kingdom of God. He specifically refers to inter-

cession for Israel, for the movement of God. Jesus is not
talking about petitions for cheese, crackers or Cadil-
lacs. This parable concerns the coming of the Lord. The
widow represents the Church in intercession.

*Then the Lord said, "Hear what the unjust judge said.
And shall God not avenge His own elect who cry out day
and night to Him, though He bears long with them? I tell
you that He will avenge them speedily. Nevertheless,
when the Son of Man comes, will He really find faith on
the earth?" (Luke 18:6-8)*

What is the meaning of this scripture? The coming of
the Son of Man! Jesus' parable does not refer at all to
repetitous prayers—going back repeatedly to God
about the same matters. Begging and badgering God
only show a lack of faith. Jesus is illustrating something totally different in this parable. The more a person asks for the same things in prayer, the less he
believes. Someone says, "What about Paul? He sought
the Lord three times about the thorn in the flesh" (II
Corinthians 12:8). That was Paul's problem! If he had
heard God's answer the first time, he would never have
had to pray again. God said "no" the first time. All
Paul did was go back to God and receive two more
"no's."

Even Jesus questioned the Father concerning drinking "the cup" of His crucifixion. "Father, all things are
possible for You. Take this cup away from Me; nevertheless, not what I will, but what You will" (Mark
14:36). God said "no." Jesus had His answer immediately, but He felt the same weaknesses that many

people do. The more we pray over our own desires, the less we receive from God. We should learn to accept God's first answer. If we learn that submission, we release a new power and faith within our hearts.

Fasting is also often misunderstood. People use fasting to twist God's arm. They say they are fasting when actually they only declare a hunger strike. "Well, I am not going to eat until—." That attitude just wastes a lot of good eating—it never moves God's heart. Fasting prepares us to receive God's commands. We do not command God. We say, "God, take me safely to the office this morning," and we expect God to reply, "Yes, sir!" "God, when I get to the office, I want to find a good parking place." "Yes, sir!" "Be sure, God, that you give me a raise today." God says, "Yes, sir!" In some immature concepts of God, He spends all His time "serving" us.

We do not understand intercession. Prayer and fasting prepare our spirits to receive and do His will. "Jesus, Your Spirit is in me. Tell me what to do now. I will begin to implement Your will." Needs in a local body of believers would be met if they stopped praying, "Oh, God, I heard that Bill is out of work. God, will you give him a job?" And God says, "Bill's situation is the reason I have you there. You give him a job!" We ask God to do things that He has empowered us to do. Prayer says, "I report in this morning, God. Now what can I do for You today?" God does not need to be informed of our needs. God says, "Before you ask, I know your needs, so do not worry." If we are the pleasure of God, He will always take care of us.

Parents waste their time praying for the salvation of their children if they are not being "God's pleasure" themselves—one who is in covenant with God. Parents should check their own relationship with God whenever they see their children in rebellion.

"Therefore by Him let us continually offer the sacrifice of praise to God, that is, the fruit of our lips, giving thanks to His name. But do not forget to do good and to share, for with such sacrifices God is well pleased" (Hebrews 13:15-16). We want to give God the sacrifice of praise, then never sacrifice by doing anything. Prayers are answered only by our actions and attitudes. What have we shared with someone lately?

If someone knocks on the door saying, "I have some hungry children. I just thought, Brother, that I would ask if you could help me." He does not expect to hear, "God bless you. Go in peace. I am going to pray for you." Then we close the door, and get on our faces, screaming and crying, "Oh, God, do you know that those children do not have anything to eat?" Those prayers will not fill empty stomachs! God says, "Get up off your knees, go to your cupboards, get some canned food and several loaves of bread and tell that parent, 'Your prayer is answered.' " How can the Church be a standard by which God can judge the world when we do not even meet one another's needs?

To accomplish God's purpose, we must have an *"I can do"* mentality. Paul says, "I can do all things through Christ who strengthens me." Does that mean we can meet one another's needs? Does that mean that in the parameters of the Body of Christ all of our needs are met? "And my God shall supply all your needs according to His riches in glory by Christ Jesus" (Philippians 4:19).

God requires whatever we have. Refusing to give what we have is being unfaithful with provisions God has entrusted to us. On the other hand, spirituality is not giving beyond our means. That sort of offering is foolish. It indicates someone is living in an unreal world. God may want someone just to love a person needing ministry while that person worries about writing a "miracle" check. Maybe God just wants someone to be faithful in a choir while he aspires to sing in an opera. God forbid that He would put some of us in responsibilities where we'll make fools of ourselves. Learning how to use and share whatever God has given us is spiritual maturity.

Be content in the call God has given. Don't strive to be "an Oral Roberts." God wants Christians to be faithful wherever he places them. Maybe one's greatest ministry is saying to a lonely person, "God loves you." If we realized the great prices paid to become like many of God's servants whom we admire, we would be much less anxious to assume their callings. I heard Kenneth Hagan telling the story of his youth. He said, "My mother was insane. When I was eight or ten years old, I used to follow her around. We never knew when she would try to kill herself."

Some of the great spiritual men in the Church today have known severe sicknesses and devastations. God says, "Be faithful over a few things." I grieve over young ministers today who have never learned that principle. They have never learned enough faithfulness to replace a lightbulb or fix a door falling off its hinges. They say, "God, I am waiting for you to give me my 'special' ministry."

At the first church where I pastored, I would build a fire and then sit around waiting to see if anyone would come to church. Only a few women attended while the men stood outside at their cars and smoked. I did not have a car of my own, so I even had to borrow a car to get there. The roaches were big enough to bridle and ride at one church where I preached! Learn what it is to say, "God, I am going to make the most of what you have given me. I am going to spend my time in the Word. I am going to spend my energy on those few things you have given me to do. Washing hands, or washing feet, or whatever it is, Lord, I am going to be faithful." One day God will say, "You have been faithful over a few things. Now I can make you ruler over many things." Ministry doesn't happen any other way. Too many spoiled people choose ministry without understanding that the price is self-denial.

Ananias and Sapphira disobeyed God. When they walked before Peter, did he pray for them? No! Peter said to Ananias, "Why has Satan filled your heart to lie to the Holy Spirit?" Immediately Ananias fell to the floor, drawing his last breath. Peter did not pray—he just spoke. Peter's response is an example of direct communion with God. Within three hours, Sapphira came to see Peter. She had not heard what had happened to her husband. Again Peter spoke, "How is it that you agreed together to test the Spirit of the Lord?"

Sapphira also fell to the floor as she heard those words and she died at Peter's feet. That response is the result of prayer, power with God, conversation with Christ in us who can handle every situation.

Paul went to a certain island where he met a sorcerer who had deceived people with all kinds of religious exercises. Paul did not get on his face and start crying out to God, "Oh, God, here is a man who is a hypocrite, a liar, a cheat!" No, Paul simply said to the man, "You shall be blind, not seeing the sun for a period of time." Immediately darkness fell on the man (Acts 13:6-11). Yes, that response is from God, whether we like it or not, and is the result of prayer, the ability to move with God.

When Paul was in Lystra, he spoke to a man who had been crippled from his mother's womb. Paul ordered, "Stand up straight on your feet!" The man leaped up and walked. Paul was obviously "prayed up." His conversations with God were up-to-date. Paul knew close fellowship with God. He understood the authority of who he was in the Lord and he knew exactly how God wanted him to speak.

". . . many wonders and signs were done through the apostles" (Acts 2:43). God gave the apostles the authority to say "yes" and "no" to life and death. The Church is entering again into a period when God is bringing His covenant people to a level of revelation so He can judge the house of God. Then He will judge the world by the standard of the Church. This is no time for playing games with God. Christians must learn obedience even in small tasks.

The mind of Christ in us has no problem giving. The mind of Christ in us has no problem loving and forgiving. The spiritual flow in our lives is hindered whenever our own concerns or desires overpower the Christ in us. The work of the Kingdom is accomplished when we release the Christ in us.

What is intercession? Intercession comes through servants desiring God's guidance and direction. Daniel fasted and prayed for twenty-four days. He still did not receive an answer to his prayer (Daniel 10). Finally, a messenger of God came to him saying, "Do not fear, Daniel, for from the first day that you set your heart to understand, and to humble yourself before your God, your words were heard; and I have come because of your words" (Daniel 10:12). Notice, Daniel was not giving God instructions. He waited to receive instructions from God. Daniel's prayers are an example of intercession.

Intercession means taking authority away from powers and principalities. Wanting beans and potatoes and praying for houses and lands has nothing to do with intercession. Intercession binds spirits in heavenly places, releasing God's command to us. God could say, "Isaiah, I need somebody to go." Isaiah replied, "Lord, here am I; send me." He received a command. Intercession binds the spirits that keep answers— God's commands—from coming.

When intercessory ministry is active and powerful before God, we receive commands of the Holy Spirit. The Holy Spirit will say, "Go on that television station." "Come off that television station." "Buy that

212

equipment." As a pastor I am subject to intercessory prayer as I lead my congregation. The Bible says, "Pray for those in authority over you." Christians must pray for those who make decisions in the Church or they will make some bad decisions. We are His servants, His army, and He is our Father. We are under command to Him. To keep commands coming from God, intercession must become a way of life.

After Anna prayed, "God, your command must come 'in the fullness of time,'" God could say, "Mary, now is the time for a son to be born."

Isaiah said, "Here am I." Mary said, "I am the handmaiden of the Lord. Be it unto me according to Your will." That submissive spirit is not the kind of prayer I hear so often today. "Oh, God, I need that; I need this." No! No! No! When we say like Mary, "Oh, God, I am your handmaiden," the commands of God are released. Jesus said to pray, "Thy will be done on earth even as it is in heaven." Out of heavenly commands, God's will is done. Prayer looses God's ability to command willing, servant spirits.

"Lord, where would you have me to go?" Saul asked when confronted by God on the road to Damascus. "Lord, what would you have me to do?" When we begin to understand submission in conversation with God, we say, "God, what do you want me to do in this circumstance?" A submissive spirit always answers the law's requirements. Paul said, "Walk in the Spirit, and you shall not fulfill the lust of the flesh" (Galatians 5:16). We never worry about falling into adultery because our minds are not given to lust. We don't worry about killing because our minds are not given to hate. If Christ is in us, the law is dead. Now we walk in close relationship with Christ. When we sing songs about Christ, tears come to our eyes. In that intimate relationship we say, "Oh, I want to see Him! I want to look upon His face!" Like a lover who has been away, we long just to see Him. Won't it be wonderful to share His presence? Won't it be wonderful when the Bridegroom comes again? He is coming to those who are longing and waiting for Him to come! If we have that intimate relationship with Him, He recognizes our needs. We do not even have to ask Him for anything. He knows!

The secret of prayer is an intimate relationship with God. In that relationship, we will want to be God's pleasure. We will ask, "What does He want to do with money He has given me?" "What does God want to do with my life and my talents?" Prayer is not telling God what we will do or asking Him for His approval. We ask God what He wants us to do, then we follow His directions. A million miles separate those two attitudes of prayer. One says, "Lord, I am ready to go." The other says, "Lord, will You approve this action I am taking?" The closer we get to God, the more we walk in His Spirit. We have no problem giving if His mind is in us. His hand reaches down and controls our billfolds. His heart loves and ministers to others through us.

Prayer depends upon relationship. We must become His pleasure. We become adulterers when we try to follow our own pleasures as well as the pleasure of His Spirit. We cannot follow both. Jesus said, "Seek first the Kingdom of God." He said, "Before you ask, I

214

know." I have had experiences when I sensed what those whom God has given to my ministry were feeling even though they were hundreds of miles away. I sensed danger wherever they were. I am just a man with the spirit of a man, but I sensed their circumstances in my own spirit. Think how much the Christ Spirit in us knows our hearts. When we are in that intimate relationship, He knows our needs.

God knows when we need encouragement. Christ in us sometimes prompts us to pick up the telephone and call a person in near or distant places. Our obedience to the Spirit is confirmed when we hear them say, "I was just sitting here contemplating suicide." Christ in us gives commands. Jesus said, "Weep with those who weep. Rejoice with those who rejoice." We are baptized into one another. When we have that experience alive in us, we live in a different dimension than the world. We cannot help but love and respond to one another because we function in body relationships.

The prophets of Baal cried and cut themselves. Elijah simply walked around saying, "Go ahead! Cry a little louder! Scream and yell!" Elijah had been hiding at the Brook of Cherith in intimate fellowship with God (I Kings 17:3). Every command of God had to be in this prophet's inner spirit. After the prophets of Baal finished crying and screaming, Elijah walked over and said, "Now, God, I am Your servant. If I am in the right relationship with You, if I am Your prophet, open the windows of heaven and send down the fire." That was all there was to it! The heavens opened, a flash of lightning came down and the altars began to burn.

215

Why? Elijah knew who he was in God. His relationship was right. He was not under some heavy cloud of guilt. He was not walking outside of God's covenant and God's provisions.

I have seen people cry and scream out to God over dying children or members of their families. God was not within a million miles of their prayers. They thought they should pray for answers, but effective prayer depends upon relationship. "Behold, the Lord's hand is not shortened, that it cannot save; nor His ear heavy, that it cannot hear. **But** your iniquities have separated you from your God" (Isaiah 59:1-2).

Jesus stood at the tomb of Lazarus and began to weep. He could feel all the pains of death down through the centuries. Jesus raised Lazarus from the dead, but notice how He did it. Jesus said, "Father, I do not need to say anything to You. In order for these people standing here to understand that I do nothing of Myself and we are in relationship—You and I are one and that relationship gives me the right to say this—I shall say, 'Lazarus, rise up.' " The tomb started shaking. The doors flew open. Out came Lazarus by the power of God's command. Jesus knew who He was!

The Kingdom awaits. Christ in us awaits. We must understand how to receive command, understand the place of intercession before God, understand the difference between asking for our pleasure and for God's pleasure. What releases His Kingdom? One little word called "faith," activating God's will in us by obeying His voice. We must move on what we know to do. Instead of asking things from God, we become God's answer to prayer. God always uses us to answer His own desires when we are His pleasure. Christ in us, the hope of glory!

12

WHEN WILL GOD MOVE AGAIN?

We are encompassed around about with a great cloud of witnesses (Hebrews 12:1). My sister, Joan, and other saints who have gone to be with the Lord are that great cloud of witnesses. Everything in glory awaits our witness on planet earth. Christians have thought that we must wait to see what God will say from the heavenlies. No! God has already spoken. God will not make another major move until His Church demonstrates the character of Christ on the earth. The great cloud of witnesses in glory await the maturing of the body of Christ. They wait, groaning, longing for the manifestation of the sons of God. They wait to see which generation will accomplish God's purposes on earth.

God's character is revealed by the patterns in which He moves. God moves by dimension. God's worship patterns began through the tabernacle, then the temple. Today His worship patterns are implemented through man, His "temple not made with hands." In the Old Testament, lambs were slain as a blood sacrifice. In the New Testament, the Lamb of God, Jesus Christ, fulfilled the necessity of blood sacrifices through His death on the cross. Today we offer praise and worship to the worthy Lamb. God always moves in patterns. Each move that God has made has drawn man's heart and spirit more and more into His purposes.

Understanding that God moves in patterns explains the purpose of the Bible. The Bible is not a "sacred" book in itself. The Bible is sacred only in giving us truth about the way God moves. The patterns and designs of God are revealed in this book. When we understand—through reading the Bible—how God moves and does His work, His purposes are made clear and we walk in light. We become sons of light as God enlightens us through revelation.

When will God move again? What circumstances recorded in the Bible caused God to move in the past? The Bible says that He is the same yesterday, today and forever. Whatever conditions caused God to move in the Old Testament and the New Testament will cause Him to move in these last days. God's patterns don't change. Christians need to study the conditions that cause God to move.

The first move of God was because the earth was

without form and void. Darkness covered the deep. Without a need for God's intervention, He would not have moved. Emptiness covered the earth because some state of life had ended. We know that life had existed because God told Adam and Eve to "multiply and replenish." The word "replenish" suggests something had been depleted. Man in the Garden was a new beginning to some event that had left the earth without form and void.

We can only speculate concerning whatever existed upon the earth before the Garden. We do know that rebellion erupted in heavenly places. Lucifer and a third of his cohorts were cast down to the earth (Isaiah 14:12-15). Apparently God designated that those spirits be confined to a certain place in order to deal with their rebellion. I believe that the spirits who were cast out of heavenly places to the earth made the planet a wilderness of spiritual rebellion. The formlessness of the earth existed because rebellious spirits were here. God was unwilling to allow that void, that lack of purpose to continue.

God planned for another confrontation, a new battleground. God's confrontation against rebellion was His creation, which was an antidote for an empty world. Even human lives, empty and without purpose, can be brought to a new level of order and purpose through the creative power of God.

The Spirit of God only moves to meet needs of creation. God moves in response to His universe. The universe is the Lord's. When the Spirit of God moves, He brings light. Creative processes immediately bring

221

illumination. The New Testament says that the true Light, Jesus Christ, came to give light to every man who comes into the world (John 1:9). The first move of God was His light shining upon one little place, the Garden of Eden.

The earth was inhabited by rebellious spirits who had no purpose. Rebellious spirits always lack purpose. They react to people who have purpose by attempting to defeat God's call in their lives. God created purpose in the midst of rebellion. He made Adam and Eve to bring order, take dominion, subdue the earth and begin to capture Satan's strongholds. Adam and Eve in the Garden were God's hope in the earth.

Man, God's offspring, must be under God's command. Otherwise, God cannot bring order to this earth. The concept of spiritual authority is battled in the Christian Church today. When one talks about submission, rebellion explodes immediately. God placed man under orders to multiply, replenish the earth, take dominion and subdue the earth. The only place under God's dominion at that time was the Garden, given to Adam and Eve. Spirits still controlled the earth, but God told Adam and Eve to subdue them.

Man failed. I believe that Adam could have subdued the earth and returned it to God's design, but Lucifer crept into the Garden from outer darkness in the form of a beautiful snake. Lucifer was the most beautiful creature that Adam and Eve had ever seen. God always teaches His people by what they see. The spirit of Satan causes us to consider "how we look" to people. Adam and Eve were impressed with Lucifer's beauty. Lucifer asked Eve if the Lord had spoken to her. When she answered "yes," Lucifer told her that God had also spoken to him. Satan always begins with that approach. Miriam and Aaron agreed that if the Lord had spoken to Moses, He had also spoken to them.

Lucifer told Adam and Eve that their eyes would be opened if they ate the forbidden fruit. Deception! Deception must be totally exposed. Paradise was destroyed because of deception. Jesus said that in the last days people will be in danger from that same power. Because of Lucifer's power, Eve was tempted and caused Adam to follow her in sin. The first move of God ended in the creation process.

Dimension number two began. "I will put enmity between you and the woman" (Genesis 3:15). God cursed Satan as man's inner conflicts began: wars in his thoughts, jealousies, strife and lust. Clashes between the forces of good and evil characterize human history.

The second conflict was between the seed of the woman and Satan's seed. Satan's seed on earth begins in rebellion. God's seed on earth begins in obedience. Rebellion cannot exist until one has received some light. Many rebellious people go to church. Rebellious people are simply those who have refused spiritual light. Unsaved people of the world are not necessarily rebellious; they are simply living in darkness.

God said that Satan would "bruise the heel of the woman." That bruising fills hospitals with physically and mentally ill people and causes other dreadful infirmities. But God gave the greatest promise in the Bible when He said that "the seed of the woman" shall bruise Satan's head. "And I will put enmity between you and the woman, and between your seed and her Seed; He shall bruise your head, and you shall bruise His heel" (Genesis 3:15). The blow to Satan's head is the terminal blow of God against all rebellion in creation.

Abraham had Isaac, Isaac had Jacob, and Jacob had twelve sons, the twelve tribes of Israel. God continued to speak through His prophets. The Seed who was to open the promises made to Abraham, making his descendants number as the stars of the sky and the sands of the sea, was yet to come.

> *Brethren, I speak as the manner of men: Though it is only a man's covenant, yet if it is confirmed, no one annuls or adds to it. Now to Abraham and his Seed were the promises made. He does not say, "And to seeds," as of many, but as of one, "And to your Seed," who is Christ. And this I say, that the law, which was four hundred and thirty years later, cannot annul the covenant that was confirmed before by God in Christ, that it should make the promise of no effect. For if the inheritance is of the law, it is no longer a promise; but God gave it to Abraham by promise. (Galatians 3:15-18)*

God seeks a people who understand that His covenant with Abraham was fulfilled in Christ. Spiritual Israel is His Church. We, the Body of Christ, are Abraham's seed. We number like the sands of the sea and the stars of heaven. We are becoming "a people who were not a people" (Romans 9:25-26).

The next great move of God following creation was the incarnation of God in human flesh. Christ became the incarnation of God, the promised Seed. God came to the world in the flesh so that He might see creation with natural understanding. That event was a move of God. The Spirit of the Lord moved upon Mary, whom God found to be a receptive, obedient vessel. Because Mary was obedient to the heavenly Father, God made her "the mother of God." I realize that statement is controversial, but the Bible teaches that Mary became "the mother of God" through her obedience.

Everything that Jesus did as the Seed of God was to establish a new order. Jesus' flesh at Gethsemane did not want to go to the cross, but He submitted His will to God. When we learn to demonstrate that principle, we also become a seed of promise. Upon the cross, with the power within His grasp to call ten thousand angels, He cried, "My God, why have You forsaken Me?" He felt the weight of the sins of all mankind in those moments of separation from the Father.

We have victory today because Jesus endured the cross. When He said, "It is finished," His mission was completed. Then came His resurrection. Did He stay in the tomb? Do death, hell and the grave have power over the spiritual seed? Jesus broke the bondage of the flesh. He snatched the keys of death, hell and the grave (Revelation 1:18) from the hand of Satan and burst forth out of the tomb! We cry, "He's risen! Our victory is final in Jesus Christ!"

Moses returned from receiving the ten commandments to find a disobedient people worshipping "golden calves." Today people worship their own "golden calves." Worship of "things" becomes a stumbling block to others. We do not belong to ourselves. We have been purchased through the death of Jesus Christ, the precious sacrifice for our sins.

As long as the law was in effect, the prophets prophesied within the parameters of the law. Then John, a new breed of prophet, came prophesying beyond the law. "Behold, the Lamb of God who takes away the sin of the world!" (John 1:29). Only then could Jesus teach that the law of old required physical restraint, but sin is actually committed in the heart (Matthew 5:21-22). The old law is dead. Some people try to resurrect it and soothe their guilt by keeping some of the laws. They feel good because they have "kept all the laws." Jesus brought God's requirements to a new dimension of the Spirit.

While the law was in effect, the prophets were restricted to prophesy within its parameters. They could prophesy of hope beyond the commandments, but they dealt with people according to the law. John began preaching the Kingdom of God, a new basis of relationship extending from God's promises to Abraham. Those promises are established through faith—like the relationship between God and Abraham.

The first accomplishment through the incarnation was that God came to the world in the flesh. Secondly, He became the firstfruit of many brethren. He was the first of a new order, a new kind of men. Thirdly, Jesus provided "the Way," not "a way." He became the chief cornerstone. Finally, the Seed of Abraham became a reality. What was once "spiritual seed" is now reality.

After the incarnation, God's next great move was fulfilling the promise spoken through the prophet Joel.

Then He said to them, "These are the words that I spoke to you while I was still with you, that all things must be fulfilled which were written in the Law of Moses and the Prophets and the Psalms concerning Me." And He opened their understanding, that they might comprehend the Scriptures. Then He said to them, "Thus it is written, and thus it was necessary for the Christ to suffer and to rise from the dead the third day, and that repentance and remission of sins should be preached in His name to all nations, beginning at Jerusalem. And you are witnesses of these things. Behold, I send the Promise of My Father upon you; but tarry in the city of Jerusalem until you are endued with power from on high." (Luke 24:44-49)

God's next great move was the enduement of power. The Seed, Jesus Christ, multiplied Himself by sending the Holy Spirit to indwell His followers. People were made mature enough to receive further truth (Matthew 16:13).

"He will glorify me, for He will take of what is mine and declare it to you. All things that the Father has are mine. Therefore I said that He will take of Mine and declare it to you" (John 16:14-15). Every characteristic that is "like Christ" can be transferred to us by the Holy Spirit.

This great move of God to place the Holy Spirit within us makes us become the incarnation of God. The seed begins to grow within individuals, and grows corporately into a tremendous Church. "If you love me, keep my commandments. And I will pray the Father, and He will send you another Helper, that He may abide with you forever, even the Spirit of truth, whom the world cannot receive" (John 14:15-17).The world cannot receive "Christ in us." The Holy Spirit came to put Christ in us—not just to make us talk in tongues. Tongues are simply the evidence that Jesus resides within us.

"The Spirit of truth, whom the world cannot receive, because it neither sees Him nor knows Him; but you know Him, for He dwells with you and will be in you" (John 14:17). Pentecost was the next move of God to make the power of Christ resident within us.

Jesus cannot come until the apostolic ministry is re-established. We are now in the period of the prophets. Today God is raising up prophets who are under the anointing of God, but the period of the apostolic ministry will soon return also. Only then can Jesus Christ come again.

I now rejoice in my sufferings for you, and fill up in my flesh what is lacking in the afflictions of Christ, for the sake of His body, which is the church, of which I became a minister according to the stewardship from God which was given to me for you, to fulfill the word of God, the mystery which has been hidden from ages and from generations, but now has been revealed to His saints. To them God willed to make known what are the riches of the glory of this mystery among the Gentiles: which is Christ in you, the hope of glory. Him we preach, warning every man and teaching every man in all wisdom, that we may present every man perfect in Christ Jesus. (Colossians 1:24-28)

Paul said that he suffered what Christ did not suffer. "Christ in us" is God's continuing incarnation. We are His continuing suffering. The Church is Christ's body, the incarnation of Christ today. The mystery which has been hidden but is now revealed to His saints is "Christ in you, the hope of glory." The mystery of this generation is Christ in us! We have never understood that mystery fully. We pray to a "God beyond the clouds in heavenly places" when Christ is in us. The hope of glory is not in the heavenlies—the "hope of the heavenlies" is on earth! Every departed saint is gathered, waiting to see how many of us are going to receive understanding and bring Christ from the heavenlies. They are waiting for total redemption as we are.

Now hope does not disappoint, because the love of God has been poured out in our hearts by the Holy Spirit who was given to us. (Romans 5:5)

If God's love is going to be manifested on planet earth, who is going to demonstrate it? Christ in us, the hope of glory. God has no other place to show His love except through His Body.

For this reason I bow my knees to the Father of our Lord Jesus Christ, from whom the whole family in heaven and earth is named, that He would grant you, according to the riches of His glory, to be strengthened with might through His Spirit in the inner man, that Christ may dwell in your hearts through faith; that you, being rooted and grounded in love, may be able to comprehend with all the saints what is the width and length and depth and height—to know the love of Christ which passes knowledge; that you

229

may be filled with all the fullness of God. Now to Him who is able to do exceedingly abundantly above all that we ask or think, according to the power that works in us, to Him be glory in the church by Christ Jesus throughout all ages, world without end. Amen. (Ephesians 3:14-21)

Many evangelicals and conservative religious people continue to be sympathetic toward national Israel as God's chosen people. This concept denies that Jesus Christ is the chief cornerstone. These Christians patronize people who deny that Jesus is the Christ. No wonder the world is in deception. No wonder God waits, grieved and lonely. God's own people make concessions to those who don't understand that Jesus Christ is the only means to God. Jesus Christ is "the" way.

In Him you also trusted, after you heard the word of truth, the gospel of your salvation; in whom also, having believed, you were sealed with the Holy Spirit of promise, who is the guarantee of our inheritance until the redemption of the purchased possession, to the praise of His glory. (Ephesians 1:13-14)

The guarantee that we are His purchased possession is the Holy Spirit. The Holy Spirit is the common denominator between heaven and earth. We communicate with God through the Spirit.

. . . that He might present it to Himself a glorious church, not having spot or wrinkle or any such thing, but that it should be holy and without blemish. (Ephesians 5:27)

The purpose of every move of God is to produce the mature Bride: Christ in us, the power of God's authority displayed through us, taking dominion of this planet. God waits for us to complete His plan. God cannot move again until we fulfill our mission on earth.

What was accomplished by the advent of the Holy Spirit? Every aspect of this teaching should be broken down and taught from house to house:

First, the Holy Spirit placed Christ in us and made us partakers of His nature. We have been bought with a price. We no longer belong to ourselves. Important decisions must be made under spiritual authority. If one refuses to do that, how will he ever trust God's voice? If we do not recognize God in the flesh, we cannot recognize God in the heavenlies.

Secondly, a new creation was established.

> *. . . that you put off, concerning your former conduct, the old man which grows corrupt according to the deceitful lusts, and be renewed in the spirit of your mind, and that you put on the new man which was created according to God, in righteousness and true holiness (Ephesians 4:22-24).*

A new creation has been formed through God. The Holy Spirit in us creates a new man with the mind of Christ. Our bodies are the temple of the Holy Spirit. Our feet are shod with the preparation of the gospel of peace, the sword of the Spirit is in our hands, and we hold tightly the shield of faith. We are a new creation, a new order consisting of people who know how to walk in love with light and wisdom.

Thirdly, the indwelling Holy Spirit makes us fruit-bearers. "But you shall receive power when the Holy

Spirit has come upon you; and you shall be witnesses to Me in Jerusalem, and in all Judea and Samaria, and to the end of the earth" (Acts 1:8).

"But the fruit of the Spirit is love, joy, peace, long-suffering, kindness, goodness, faithfulness, gentleness, self-control" (Galatians 5:22). Discipline cannot be separated from the fruit of the Spirit. Spiritual fruit cannot be resident in us until we know God's Word and know how to pray. The fruit of the Spirit is our witness to the world. God cannot judge the world except by the fruit of our lives. Our witness must begin in our own households, then extend to the workplace, social activities, etc.

Jesus was thirty years old and still subject to His parents. Many parents release their children before they can possibly make the right choices. God taught me a great lesson recently when I shared with an elderly couple. One spirit had been subject to authority in former years. Another spirit has never known submission to anyone—including husband, family or church.

This wife controlled the family with her illnesses and emotions. I listened carefully to this woman whom spirits had driven almost insane. She said, "I don't know that man. I am not going to bed with him." I turned in a few moments to him and said, "Sir, you go to bed." Immediately, he got up and went to bed. His spirit knew what it was to be under control in submission. Then I said to her, "Now it is time for you to go to bed." She said, "You are not going to tell me what to do. Who do you think you are? I am much older than you are. You can't tell me anything." God said to me, "See the difference?" We must submit to God. The scripture says to "obey those over you in the Lord." God gives us areas of trust to test our submission.

God has appointed apostles, prophets, evangelists, pastors and teachers for the equipping and perfecting of the saints until they come to the full stature of Christ, until they are mature and the Bride of Christ is complete (Ephesians 4:11-16). Then Christ can join her at the marriage supper of the Lamb. The Holy Spirit gives us the potential for becoming His Bride.

Finally, the Holy Spirit gives a standard by which God can judge the world. "And when He has come, He will convict the world . . ." (John 16:8). He will judge the world because He first established a standard in the Garden. The Garden of Eden was a prototype of the Church. When the Church reclaims that standard, God can judge the world. He cannot judge politics in the world when politics corrupt the Church. He cannot judge greed in the world as long as greed dominates the Church. He cannot judge lust in the world while lust influences the Church. God cannot judge the world when His Church is filled with people comparing themselves among themselves. God must have a Church that is mature, a demonstration of Christ.

God greatly desires to move again, but He cannot move because we restrict Him. In His omnipotent sovereignty, God limited Himself in His plan of operation in His Church. That is the reason the "hope of glory" is in us.

God moved in creation as an answer to a world needing order. He moved in the incarnation to show Himself
in the flesh to the world. He moved in Pentecost to put
Christ in us. When will He move again? Only one more
move of God awaits. That move of God will bring
Christ back to judge the earth.

When will God move again? When the last move that
God began at Pentecost is completed. "Go into all the
world and preach the gospel to every creature. He that
believes and is baptized shall be saved." The gospel of
the Kingdom must be demonstrated. A vast number of
preachers on television proclaim "Jesus Christ," but
we are doing poorly in demonstrating His message.
Christ in us must take dominion over the earth.

The Holy Spirit in us makes the earth God's footstool. The next move of God cannot occur until Christ
in us takes dominion. I have not seen a full demonstration. I have seen only bits and pieces of Kingdom
authority and dominion. The answer does not lie
within great numbers of people in unity. Two or three in
agreement on planet earth will be able to begin demonstrating that necessary witness.

Secondly, God will move again when we become that
standard by which God can judge the earth. "And God
judged the harlot" (Revelations 19:2). How did God
judge the harlot church? God compared the harlot
Church with a pure Bride. God can say to the harlot,
"See, it can be done! My Bride heard and followed
truth. She followed the revelation I gave her."

Thirdly, God will move again when His family upon

planet earth becomes one. Jesus said, "Father, make them one so the world may know" (John 17:21). Few have understood that prayer. Oneness will be a new emphasis in theology when we understand that God's Church is the standard used to judge the world. Jesus said, " I pray that they become one, so the world may know and be judged." The ultimate end, the culmination of the ages, is that "everything in heaven and in earth may become one" in Jesus Christ (Ephesians 1:10).

God will move again when the family on earth and in heaven become one. A new heaven and new earth can come "wherein dwells righteousness." The tabernacle of God will dwell with men. There will be no need for light because the Lamb Himself will be the Light. There will be no need for the temple because we are God's temples. The Bride, without spot and wrinkle, can stand in unity, in faith and know how to release the Christ in her with power. Then God can say, "That is enough! I have a witness! I have a witness!" (Revelation 21:22-23).

The next move of God will unite His Son in marriage. The marriage supper of the Lamb, the completion of establishing the Kingdom, the eternal rule of God, will finally take place. God will rule and reign completely without rebellion. All rebellion will be put down and everything will operate in proper structure, order and design before God. God wants an orderly Church to demonstrate proper structure to the world. Rebellion in the Church hinders that final move of God.

The Kingdom of God will be presented to Christ by

the Kingdom prototype, a true demonstration of Him in the world. When His Kingdom on earth has been demonstrated in prototype, Christ will return. "Eye has not seen nor ear heard" of anything like the glorious universe that God has planned for us from the beginning, the ultimate reward for those who have demonstrated the Kingdom of God on earth.

ABOUT THE AUTHOR

Bishop Earl Paulk is senior pastor of Chapel Hill Harvester Church located in Atlanta, Georgia. Chapel Hill Harvester Church has eighteen full-time pastors serving a local parish of over four thousand people with thousands more receiving ministry by television and outreach ministries.

Bishop Paulk grew up in a classical Pentecostal family as the son of Earl P. Paulk Sr., a former assistant general overseer of the Church of God. His grandfather, Elisha Paulk, was a Freewill Baptist preacher.

Personal and educational exposure have given Bishop Paulk an ecumenical understanding enjoyed by few church leaders in the world today. He earned a Bachelor of Arts degree from Furman University which is a Baptist institution, and a Masters of Divinity degree from Candler School of Theology which is a Methodist seminary.

Earl Paulk was named to the office of Bishop in the International Communion of Charismatic Churches in 1982. He assumes oversight of many churches, directly and indirectly influenced by the ministry of Chapel Hill Harvester Church. The church hosts an annual Pastors' Conference in which leaders from local churches across the nation absorb anointed teaching, observe ministry demonstration and have the opportunity for personal dialogue on the major concerns confronting the Church today.

Under Bishop Paulk's leadership, Chapel Hill Harvester Church has become a successful working prototype of a true Kingdom Church. The foundation of the church is Kingdom principles applied to the Biblical concept of a City of Refuge.

The church ministries include a home for unwed mothers; a licensed child placement agency; ministry to those chemically addicted and their families; a ministry to those wishing to come out of the homosexual community; outreach programs to nursing homes, prisons, and home-bound individuals; Alpha, one of the most widely acclaimed youth ministries in the nation; and many other ministries designed to meet the needs of the Body of Christ.

Television outreach includes the **Harvester Hour** and the **K-Dimension** programs seen weekly on P.T.L. Satellite Network and on numerous other television broadcasts nationwide.

Chapel Hill Harvester Church is the tangible expression of God's love through the visionary efforts of Bishop Earl Paulk, his wife, Norma, and founding pastors Don and Clariece Paulk.

Other books by Earl Paulk

The Wounded Body of Christ
Satan Unmasked
Sex Is God's Idea
The Betrothed
Ultimate Kingdom
The Divine Runner

For further information please contact—

P.O. Box 7300 • Atlanta, GA 30357